Sea of Love
Sea of Loss

LETTERS TO OLIVE

For Sharon
A story from the heart

John Dunn

**Praise for *A Letter to Olive*, the radio programme
first broadcast on Easter Sunday, 31st March, 2002**

"I have wept with you, laughed with you and wondered at the
depth of love that can be hidden in what we call 'trivia'…"

✤

"Your programme is like a bunch of roses given to me,
I delight in its beauty, as it gives me courage."

✤

"Your programme about Olive was *wonderful*. Will you publish it?
It was so touching – truly it was…" Maeve Binchy

✤

"I've listened to it several times. It is simply one of the most moving,
honest and ultimately life-affirming pieces of radio I've ever heard."

✤

"I've never heard anything more sincere, more honest,
or more meaningful at the death of a spouse. Frankly, I think it should
[be] played at every wedding and every anniversary thereafter…"

✤

"Thank you for sharing your journey. It has helped us to express love to each other now in a way that we can *always* hold…"

✤

"You have done many a public service; for myself, it has brought into sharp focus how much my own wife means to me and how I should treasure our togetherness all the more…"

✤

"My heart was breaking… It was such a wonderful 'letter' and love story… so alive and real…"

✤

"You exquisitely capture the transcendent dimension of the quotidian, the bits and pieces of every day that only acquire deeper significance when the loved one is gone forever…"

✤

"Your sharing your loss gave us an opportunity to say how much we appreciate our being together and happy…"

✤

"Your loss may be slightly compensated by the joy you have
given many people with the programme…"

❖

"'The seed in your heart shall blossom' – never were truer words spoken.
I believe that seed was planted in many hearts on Sunday night – and will
grow in many hearts, and will bear much fruit…"

❖

"Thank you for being so brave and allowing the whole
of Ireland into your heart…"

❖

"The sense of absolute reality overlaid with true emotion and
feelings expressed so honestly and freely were truly awesome…"

❖

"How refreshing and how healing to have a man to speak about
what is closest to his heart. I think, I hope, you may have opened the
floodgates for those following you…"

❖

About the Author

John Quinn is a well-known broadcaster who retired from RTÉ Radio in December 2002 after a career of twenty-five years, during which he won various awards at home and in Tokyo and New York.

An established writer of children's fiction (he won the Bisto Book of the Year Award in 1992) he has also edited several other acclaimed publications.

In February 2003, he was awarded an honorary D.Litt by the University of Limerick.

Sea of Love
Sea of Loss

LETTERS TO OLIVE

John Quinn

**TOWN
HOUSE**
DUBLIN

First published in 2003 by

TownHouse, Dublin
THCH Ltd
Trinity House
Charleston Road
Ranelagh
Dublin 6
Ireland

1 2 3 4 5 6 7 8 9 10

A CIP catalogue record for this book is available from the British Library.

ISBN: 1-86059-173-6

Cover and text design by Anú Design, Tara
Typeset by Anú Design, Tara
Printed by Mackays of Chatham Ltd, Chatham, Kent

Contents

For you, Eddie Duchins, who else?
Love you, miss you — above all, thank you.

Acknowledgements

My thanks to:

- Pat Hunt, who started the whole thing off by asking me to 'write a piece on love and loss' for the Christmas 2001 newsletter of the Holy Redeemer Parish, Bray, Co. Wicklow, and also for his subsequent, moving, obituary in *The Irish Times*.

- *The Irish Times* for permission to reproduce Olive's obituary.

- Aidan Matthews for permission to reproduce his beautiful poem 'Watercolour for a Widower'. A line from that poem gave us the title for this book.

- Ann Henning Jocelyn for permission to reproduce an extract from her collection *Keylines*.

● Michael Campion, sound operator at RTÉ Radio, whose skill and sensitivity were so important in the making of the radio programme *A Letter to Olive*.

● The hundreds of listeners who wrote in response to that programme, many of them (notably Maeve Binchy) pleading with me to publish the story in book form.

● Anne O'Neill, who typed the manuscript and encouraged me to write it in the first place.

● Treasa Coady of TownHouse who saw the possibility of a book in the story and who with Marie Heaney and Claire Rourke helped me realise that possibility with their guidance and suggestions.

John Quinn
March 2003

And it was lovely then
And you were lovely then
And we were young
And so in love
And it was lovely then

Prologue

5 a.m. Friday, 29th June, 2001

Dawn has broken over Bray. I cannot sleep, so I will write. Dawn has also stolen in from the Irish Sea and crept over Shanganagh Cemetery, just outside Bray, over a new flower-laden grave. My dozen red roses lie on the resting place of my darling Olive Rosemary McKeever, my wife of thirty-three years. It is the end of the most unimaginably traumatic week of my life – unreal, surreal, unbelievable – my beautiful one left me just eighty-four hours ago, at 5 p.m. on Monday, 25th June.

It was Christmas postponed. Just before Christmas 2000, Olive had a horrific fall down a stone stairs, broke her neck, and lost her swallow in the trauma of the fall. She was hospitalised for three months, incarcerated in a monstrous metal head-frame – euphemistically called a halo. Given that there was no guarantee that she would ever recover her swallow, Olive was, understandably, suicidal that Christmas. 'This is not Christmas,' I told her. 'Christmas will be when you are better.' And she did get better. Ever a fighter, she recovered her swallow and finally shed the halo. But, four days after Olive came out of hospital, her sister Derry died unexpectedly. After all that trauma, Olive deserved a mid-summer Christmas. I booked us into the Great Southern Hotel in Rosslare for two nights, and then into Kelly's on the Strand for six nights. Rosslare has always had a special place in our hearts. When the children were small, we rented a holiday home there for the month of July for successive years. To be going back now and staying in Kelly's … Olive was so excited. I must not tell anyone where we were going … it was to be our secret.

After a very pleasant stay in the Great Southern, we moved into Kelly's on the Sunday afternoon with a mountain of luggage. *[Will I ever forget the number of outfits you brought?]* We checked into our room at 4 p.m. – just in time to watch Meath's resounding victory over Kildare in the Leinster Senior Football Championship.

Olive couldn't bear to watch the game, as usual, but rejoiced in the win, and was so happy when she rang our son, Declan, that evening. We went for a walk on the beach before our first dinner in Kelly's – for which, of course, Olive dressed in head-turning elegance. A Guinness and a port in the bar, and then to bed. For once, Olive slept well and enjoyed breakfast in bed while I savoured the Monday papers.

It was a warm, humid day. This would be the Alternative Christmas Day. There would be champagne for dinner tonight … We relaxed in the hotel garden. You sipped a Tio Pepe while I read from Ben Kiely's *Collected Stories*. Lunchtime. You chided me for going for the full lunch, while you had a bowl of soup and a glass of Guinness. It was leek and potato soup, as I remember. It was a happy lunch. I asked you were you glad you came … we were just getting into the swing of things. It was Christmas Day.

Back to the garden. We move to the shelter of the 'teahouse'. Sound of the surf as we relaxed again. I read Ben Kiely's story 'A Cow in the House'. You're determined to have that first swim – and in the sea, not in the pool. You send me down to the pool for a towel. *[I sneak an afternoon tea while I'm there!]* You put on your swimsuit and a shower cap. I should really go with you, but I have no togs with me. I help you over the rope. You lean on me as I guide you down the dune. [*It is the last time I will hold your living hand.*] You say, 'I'll probably be back in a minute if the water is too cold.' I go back up and watch closely as you wade gingerly into the sea. I can imagine your 'ooohs' as you hit water … you find a depth and go down. I can see your arms do the breast-stroke. Once, twice, thrice, maybe. Then nothing. Your head stays face down in the water. Something is wrong. Jesus – no! Please. No. I race down, call out your name. No response. I race in, drag you out, limp, unconscious. I will always remember how light you felt …

Before I reach the water's edge, others have arrived. Two doctors, a nurse, a lifeguard. They take over. I clutch your showercap, look on, helpless, disbelieving. Please, please don't go. Please let it not be true. Please. They work furiously, thumping your chest. A part of me wants to protest that they are hurting you. There is froth on your mouth. You can't be dead, but I know you are. I can do nothing. I should be talking to you, but I freeze. You lie there, limp, bedraggled, lifeless.

The ambulance men arrive. They try to resuscitate you, but it's hopeless. I can't believe it. Won't believe it. People are kind and supportive, especially Billy Kelly and Brenda Sweeney. But you're gone from me – and you never said goodbye … You are taken to the ambulance. I go with you on that nightmare journey to Wexford Hospital. What's wrong with me? I can't talk to you. I sit there and stare at you. Numb. All I can do is repeat the mantra – 'Sacred Heart of Jesus, I place her in your eternal loving care'. We reach the hospital. The casualty staff go through the motions of trying to resuscitate you. Futile. I sit by your side, stroking your arm, your bedraggled hair. The hospital chaplain gives you the Last Blessing. Everyone is so kind. Mary the nurse. Billy Kelly. Brenda and Noel Sweeney, who followed the ambulance. Then the phone calls begin. My brother Noel. Your brother Peter. It isn't happening. But it *has* happened. Eventually I leave. I kiss your lips and withdraw, reluctantly. Numb.

The curate from Rosslare arrives and sits with me. Then the phone calls I dread making to the children. Kelly's staff are wonderful, especially

Eddie Cullen, the manager. Noel arrives from Dublin. Approaching midnight, we must make that awful journey back to the hospital to identify you formally to the Gardaí and make a statement.

To the mortuary chapel. You are wheeled out – still as you were, wrapped in a sheet, your lovely hair still bedraggled. This is not the way it was meant to be. Unreal, unreal, unreal. We return to the hotel. The heavens echo to a prolonged thunderstorm and the rain comes down in torrents ...

CALM

Of course I'm calm –
On the surface.
Only a gentle ripple
Disturbs the quiet waters
Of my life.
But underneath
Deep deep down
There is turmoil.
Shadow beasts
Scythe through the gloom
Unspeakable monsters
Lurk in cavernous lairs
Among bottomless, bottomless
Depths.
So take my hand
And tread water with me
Teach me to be calm
Like when you taught
Our children to swim,
Assuage my fears
Help me to be calm
But not
Becalmed.

1

The Beginning
of the Adventure

Of course, dear reader, you remember where you were on 22nd November 1963, when an assassin's bullets echoed around the world? But can you remember where you were exactly two years later – 22nd November 1965? I can, because it was a defining day in my life.

I presented myself for admission to James Connolly Memorial Hospital, Blanchardstown, Dublin – affectionately known to its inmates as the Blanch – a sanatorium for the treatment of tuberculosis. TB had ravaged the country in the 1930s, 1940s and 1950s, before its advance was checked by developments in medicine and the building of a number of sanatoria like the Blanch. In his book, *Ireland Since the Rising*, Tim Pat Coogan notes how the slum-dwellers of Dublin gave much of the credit for this to Dr Noel Browne, TD – 'the man that gave us the free TB'.

I was a few weeks short of my twenty-fourth birthday, a primary teacher, earnest and diligent in my work and study (three weeks earlier, I had been conferred with a BA degree, pursued through evening classes), but also gauche and not very wise in the ways of the world.

In the summer of 1965, I had been on a five-week study-tour in the United States with a group of teachers. It had been a marvellous experience – three weeks residency in New York State University and two weeks on tour – Niagara, Chicago, Philadelphia and Washington. We were guests in the White House and the Capitol, meeting President Johnson, Bobby and Ted Kennedy, former President Eisenhower and many others – a once-in-a-lifetime experience, which certainly developed me socially. I remember, on the flight home, trying to arrange a date with one of the women teachers, who told me I was very talented, but that I didn't give of my talents enough and that I needed to be much more outgoing. I told her that, 'at home', I was very shy and had an inferiority complex. She refused to believe this. She also refused me the date (the 'line was engaged'), which, of course, further punctured my self-esteem.

Come September, I resumed teaching and – true to form – began studying at night in UCD for a Higher Diploma in Education. Teaching and study – and very little social life. I developed a persistent cough that caused some annoyance, but little bother otherwise. So, when the mobile X-ray unit visited Earlsfort Terrace one November evening (an indication of how real the TB threat still was), more for fun than anything else, I joined a few friends to 'have our photographs taken'. The fun quickly dissolved a week or two later when I was summoned for a second X-ray. A shadow had been detected on one lung and, even though I had no symptoms other than the cough and did not feel ill, the message was clear: I had TB and would have to spend some time in Blanchardstown. How much time was not clear. Three months? Six months? Nine? A year? It was all very uncertain and not a little unreal. It was a particularly hard blow for my mother as, a few weeks earlier, my father had been taken to hospital with a heart attack.

So, it was a somewhat bemused and nervous young man who was admitted to Ward 5, Unit 2, on that November evening, to join Dan, Jimmy, Ned, Arthur and Paddy – just in time for 'rest hour', from 5–6 p.m., followed by a 'boiled egg tea'. It was a Monday evening, so the three young men who were 'on grade' were allowed go to the weekly film show after tea. It gave me the opportunity to discuss life in the Blanch with the older men – Ned and Paddy – and, in good dutiful teacher fashion, to write out notes on my Finglas students for the benefit of my successor.

Dr Monica Clay welcomed me to Blanchardstown. Across the Atlantic Ocean, her namesake, Cassius, would successfully defend his World Heavyweight Boxing crown, while I would – hopefully – sleep.

SOMETIME, ONETIME

Sometime, onetime
When we were young
I wonder did our paths
ever cross?
In Navan maybe
At a football match,
Or in a sweetshop
– Tierney's? –
In Slane
At a McMaster pageant?
Or later –
Did you pass
St Patrick's on a bus
Airport-bound? ·
And catch a glimpse
Of a shy, awkward student
Who wondered if
Sometime, onetime
He might meet and love
Someone like you?

2

Life
in 'the Blanch'

Blanchardstown hospital was built on a similar model to other sanatoria of the 1950s – Merlin Park in Galway and Ardkeen in Waterford. Twelve forty-bed, single-storey units and a three-storey hospital building set in a wooded estate. The units were strictly segregated on a gender basis – apart from the children's unit. Treatment consisted of rest, medication – and fresh air. (It took a while to get used to ward doors on to a veranda being left open, day and night.) The regime was strict. Rest hours were hours of *rest*, regularly policed by the sister-in-charge. There was a hospital radio service available on headphones, but transistor radios were banned. This led to a constant cat-and-mouse battle between Sister and the younger patients, with regular confiscation of the offending transistors. I was lucky to escape such confiscation, and found the radio a great comfort and companion during my sojourn – little realising that, ten years later, I would launch out on a career in radio.

The rules and restrictions of sanatorium life reminded me of the boarding-school life I had left only six years previously. Of course, the regime was for our good – we were there to be made well. But when romance would later enter the equation, it proved more than frustrating. Dr Holmes, the Medical Officer, was very keen for me to continue my Higher Diploma in Education studies, and made a special appeal to UCD on my behalf. The appeal was turned down, and reading for leisure, rather than for academic ends, became more important for me. That was, of course, when I wasn't involved in exciting occupational therapy pursuits, such as the construction of fruit baskets from lollipop sticks and toy furniture from matchboxes. On a more cerebral level, French and German lessons were available on the hospital radio service but, again, this was leavened by admittedly less challenging, but more pleasurable, pursuits such as 'penny-in' games of cards and (courtesy of an understanding porter) regular wagers with the village bookmaker.

Life was slow-paced and reasonably tolerable in the Blanch. I was slowly initiated into institutional life – salt and holly leaves in my bed (shades of boarding school again). Christmas came and slowly went. It was my first Christmas away from home, and it was a lonely time. And all the time, unknown to me, just a field away in Unit 4, lay someone who would ultimately put an end to my loneliness.

Visitors did help. Even though the sanatorium was quite a distance from the city, family and work colleagues came regularly, often bearing gifts of much-sought home cooking, which relieved the predictable tedium of the hospital menu. Incredibly, the visitors regularly brought cigarettes, for this was the 1960s and most of us were regular smokers. Smoking was allowed, even though many of us were being treated for disease of the lung (including Kevin, whose lungs had been described by Dr Holmes as 'lace curtains'). Alcohol was prohibited, but that did not prevent 'fourteen dozen of stout' being consumed in Unit 2 on Christmas Eve. I, being a non-drinker, did not partake and retired to my bed with an illicit transistor. Sister had her revenge on St Stephen's Day, however, when, with all the cunning of a customs officer, she intercepted twenty-six bags of beer.

Visiting hour had its humorous moments, too. I remember an obviously fearful visitor approaching Andy from our ward with a hankie over his mouth, asking where patient so-and-so was. Quick as a flash, Andy whipped out a hankie to cover *his* mouth before giving the required information.

I have always considered my sojourn in Blanchardstown to be a major part of my education. For a raw, callow young fellow to be cast among a collection of the charming and the cantankerous, young blades and hardened 'chaws', the wise and the world-weary, and to live in close proximity with them for nine months – it could not be otherwise. I spent evenings, listening to old men recall the Dublin of their youth ('D'yis remember the Fountain Cinema?'), sharing stories and tall tales:

> Jimmy: 'I'm tellin' yis – it was a busload of skeletons!'
>
> John C: 'Must have been Christmas – they were down to a skeleton staff!'

And enduring John Coates' (a great big loveable burly Dub) permanent restlessness to be out in the world again: 'I've worked out that, while I'm in the Blanch, I'll have consumed 4,032 tablets, a five-gallon drum of Streptomycin and 779 rings of black puddin'.'

For some, the restlessness was short-lived. There were regular examples of fellows who 'did a bunk' after one night in the Blanch. They could not face up to nine months' incarceration.

For others, the outside world would never be a reality again. Paddy, in the bed next to me, died four hours after we heard the bells ring in 1966. It was my first experience of death at close hand. It was the first of a succession of deaths I would witness over the next six months.

A sort of life, painful death, laughter, tears, bonhomie, fun, friction, frustration, loneliness; they were all about me, contributing to my development, my education. And, if that were not enough, into my life on a raw March afternoon walked a vision in a black leather coat.

3

The Black
Leather Coat

Every few weeks, we were sent down by ambulance to the hospital block for a swab test – a rather indelicate exercise in which one had to cough up sputum which would then be tested for 'positive' or (hopefully) 'negative'. Indelicacy apart, we looked on the trip as a break in the routine of sanatorium life. I had been for a number of these outings in my first few months in Blanchardstown, but nothing remotely exciting had ever happened. The 1st March, 1966 would change all that. My diary records the event thus:

Then came the girls. A smasher from Unit 4 – Miss McKeever. Phhorr! Must investigate! Actually let the door close in her face as I was dashing to hear the commentary on the Leopardstown Chase ... Arkle beat Height of Fashion by a neck.

Not the most romantic circumstances for a first meeting. Not even a meeting. I don't think we even spoke to each other. I had Arkle on my mind but she *was* a smasher! Stunningly beautiful. Elegant, with the walk of a queen. And she wore a black leather coat. In a drab hospital building, where tawdry woollen dressing gowns were the mode, she wore a black leather coat. In this instance, height of fashion won at a canter!

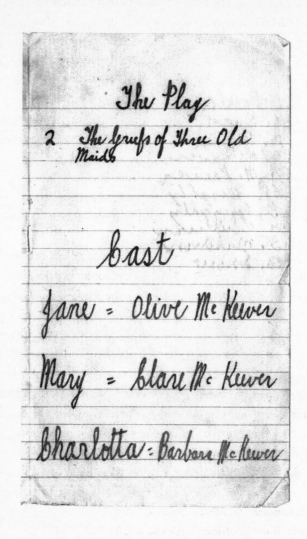

A little treasure from Olive's childhood. A handwritten 'programme' (price 2d) of an entertainment she put on for the family with her twin sisters, Barbara and Clare.

Like many an impressionable young fellow, I had fallen in and out of love with a succession of nurses during my first three months in the sanatorium. This was different. The vision in the black leather coat totally bowled me over. Miss McKeever. The only people with that surname that I was aware of were Fr McKeever, the parish priest of Trim, Co. Meath, and Peter McKeever, the former Meath footballer. How thrilled I was to discover that the former was her uncle (who, in the space of the next ten years, would marry us and baptise our three children) and the latter was her brother. A wonderful start. Further investigation elicited that she was Olive, 'a lovely girl in every way ... very bright ... speaks a number of languages ... worked in Aer Lingus and on the Cunard Line'. My elation was tempered somewhat. Out of my depth here, I thought. What interest could a glamorous, much-travelled woman like that have in a gauche, reclusive fellow like me? I was smitten. I would make an effort. But how?

We were both confined to our respective units – except for exotic swab-test outings. I made a start by putting in requests on the Tuesday request programme on the hospital radio. I soon discovered I had competition for Olive's interest. Any attempts at subtlety or coded messages went over the DJ's head. I was furious with him when he made a total mess of my brilliant (or so I thought) request of 8th March. Nelson's Pillar had been blown up the previous night. I put in a request sending 'Greetings to Charlie Parnell from Dan O'Connell and all your friends down the road. Haven't seen you for ages!' The DJ hadn't a clue what I was on about. No, a more direct approach was needed. I would be bold and write to the fair Olive. I would be even bolder – and hopefully impress the multilingual beauty – by writing in German! In German? Well, it would be a way of putting my meagre language skills to use. Amazingly, I still have the first draft of the '*brief auf Deutsch*' ... How I cringe when I read it now.

Ich komme aus Co. Meath, genau wie Sie.
[I come from Co. Meath, just like you.]

Hoffentlich höre ich bald von Ihnen.
[Hopefully I will hear from you soon.]

Yeuch! To cover all my options, I hastily wrote a second letter in English. The next problem was the postal system. I had to depend on an understanding nurse or porter to smuggle the letters into Ward 5, Unit 4 – only a field away. (How the echoes of boarding school keep creeping into this story.)

Now came the waiting period. Five days later, the reply came, addressed to 'Herr J. Quinn'. Joy of joys! It was a cautious reply, but I instantly warmed to her style, her ironic touches.

Unit 4,
Blanchardstown,
Saturday, 26th March, 1966,

Dear John,
Thank you for both your letters. The second one was not requested (who was casting aspersions on my ability to understand German!) but welcome. It saved me the effort of having to compose a missive in Deutsch!

The grapevine has obviously been hard at work. Full marks for your detection work to date regarding county of birth, place of employment, etc. Thank you for your good wishes concerning my conference next Wednesday. I do hope to get grade. Naturally, the upsetting news of the long wait to your grade and obviously interesting company has made the prospect seem not as exciting as it might be!

It's nice to know I have brought some brightness into your life. My term in Blanchardstown will not be in vain after all! Full marks for the closing line in your letter – don't intend to compete!

Olive

Note 1: I wish I could remember that closing line.
Note 2: 'Getting grade' in Blanchardstown meant that one was allowed up for walks, trips to the shop, cinema, church, etc. It was a step nearer the exit gate.

This could be the start of something big. This *was* the start of some-thing big. For the next three months, the letters would go back and forth – always addressed to *Fraulein* Olive and *Herr* John, respectively. Wonderful letters that, for a start, relieved the tedium of sanatorium life. Wonderful, wonderful letters where we gradually unfolded our personalities and learned about each other.

Olive was put on Grade 4 about a month later. She was ecstatic about being allowed out for walks. A little taste of freedom. The walks brought her around by Unit 2 on occasion, which allowed us the opportunity to exchange a wave or – even more daring – a brief few words at some dis-tance, she from the road, me leaning from the bathroom window. She would, of course, never be allowed to enter Unit 2. The only way through this frustration was to write longer and more frequent letters. Adding to the frustration were the comments of my fellow-inmates as Olive passed by. I did enjoy those of Eugene, who had recently joined us. Eugene and I shared an interest in horse-racing. He would train his (pretend) binoculars on '*Oeil d'Olive*' (as he called her) and give a Peter O'Sullevan commentary on how well the Oaks favourite was moving on the gallops this morning. As the weeks slid by, and our 'relationship' became known, the teasing increased on all sides. One nurse berated me for the distress I was causing Sr Mary Olive McKeever, Irish Sister of Charity. For a moment, she almost convinced me. But then, no Sister of Charity would sprinkle perfume on her letters to *Herr* John Quinn and write on the envelope: '*Thought it was time to have you scent again.*'

How I loved those little 'postmarks':

'Smile! It has arrived!'

'Bingo! Bingo! Bingo!'

'No Postman! Now rain! Life!!'

Paradise Island,
Wednesday, 7 p.m.

Dear John,
Ich bin sehr lustig und – *on second thoughts, bingo to the Deutsch lark! Don't feel I want to be confined by pidgin language today. I feel utterly on top of the world and see everything through a gorgeous haze. Yes, the door has begun to open – OLIVE HAS GOT GRADE!*

Why can't I hear the cheers from Unit 2? Never mind, I'm cheering enough for everyone. Eileen says if I don't stop grinning my face will never be the same again! Don't say it! On two occasions today I have trekked to the bathroom for the express purpose of signalling the news to you. What happened? Nothing – absolutely no response. In disgust I retreated to share my joy with a more receptive audience. Their enthusiasm is now beginning to wear a bit thin – hence my decision to shout my news to you. Aren't you lucky?

Oh, I have just remembered my big grudge and subsequent decision not to write again. How could you (sob!) share my tender passages with other people? (smile breaking through) In my present expansive mood I have decided to forgive you. Stop! Andy is looking over your shoulder – nasty, nasty, nasty!

Yesterday my first big thrill of the day was a letter from you. Then (my hand is shaking with emotion!) I actually saw you pass my window! Phew – it was almost too much – not quite though – why did you not come in?? No you didn't upset my meditations – only changed their general direction!

My feelings are too effervescent for expression on paper – pity you aren't here! Do you think I'm naughty? I feel wonderful, wonderful, wonderful! Must go, the celebration party is starting …

Yours sincerely,
Sister Mary Olive McKeever!!

How I loved those letters. How I suddenly loved life in the Blanch. How I was growing to love Sr Mary Olive.

Grade 4 could not come quickly enough for me. In the meantime, there was the promise of being allowed out to Mass on Easter Sunday – our first real meeting. My diary records that meeting thus:

Olive a major distraction at Easter Mass – but I tried to concentrate (on Mass!). Afterwards, the big moment! Had to introduce myself to Olive. Pat and I walked 'home' with Olive and Eileen. Far, far too little time. We talked about life in the Blanch, etc., but couldn't get down to important things. Final chat outside Unit 4. Sr Moran was on duty, so no crumpets and tea! Au revoir. Verdict – a really lovely girl – looks, manner, personality, the lot – but somehow I felt I was out of my depth! Too good for me? Although neither of us were the people we are in our letters. Again, the time was all too brief, and I must wait four more weeks till grade! However it was a big thrill. It remains to be seen what her letters will be like now! On the radio, 'Bye Bye Blues'. Enough said!

However, Olive's next letter gave me hope.

I am so glad to hear I came up to expectations – I was waiting with bated breath for the verdict! Have just remembered you said 'above expectations' – nicer still! Now what nice things can I say to you so we can form a mutual admiration society! Being honest, I found it slightly disconcerting to be confronted by someone I had been scribbling nonsense to without thought. I was lucky though, my 'unknown' correspondent was you and who could ask for anything more!! Seriously though, brief though our meeting was, I enjoyed it. Happy Easter all over again!

Olive

4

A New Life

There was another unexpected bonus outing on the Thursday after Easter. I was allowed out to attend an Easter 1916 commemoration concert. It was a terrific concert, but the best part was walking Olive 'home', huddled under an umbrella, battling against wind and rain. Oh, it was lovely, until a spoil-sport ambulance driver insisted that Olive take a lift and left me walking the streets in the rain, but not before Olive slipped me a letter. I floated home.

Unit 4,
Tuesday, 3rd May, 1966,

Dear John,
How difficult it is to come down to earth, take up my pen and write in a sober manner. Your latest missive is responsible for my present exalted state – 14 pages! I feel as if all my birthdays have come at once. The 'more, more, more – soon, soon, soon' is re-echoed a thousand times.
Am not sure what shroud you wish me to unveil – will I? won't I?

Madly daring, I begin. I was attached to the Purser's Staff of the Queen Elizabeth. *Had been at sea almost a year when the blow fell. In that period we did a Caribbean cruise (gorgeous) and an extensive Mediterranean cruise. Prior to joining Cunard I worked as a ground hostess for Aer Lingus, so in one way or another my work has always been connected with travel. My biggest thrill travel-wise was a visit to South Africa. Loved the country and climate and the great highlight was a few days spent in Kruger Park. My enjoyment was greatly tempered by the awful colour bar – the 'No Blacks Allowed' signs plastered all over the place. Came home and went through a period of reading* Late Have I Loved Thee *and* Naught for Your Comfort. *Sorry – Sorry – must not start on that subject – it makes me see red!*

Big Event of Yesterday – John actually braved the inner sanctum of Unit 4! The ensuing excitement – the quickened heartbeats! – but we would still like more. One fly in the ointment – it wasn't Olive he came to see! No – alack and alas – another rival comes into the picture [I was delivering a textbook to a fellow-patient Colette]. *Can I bear it? – that is the question.*

Mary has just come back from her conference and she goes home on Saturday. Ward 5 has gone mad! Talking of conferences brings to mind yours – between crossing fingers and curling toes (do you ever curl your toes?), daily treks to the church and all my pennies going on candles – well you just have to get grade! Sudden thought – perhaps I'm overdoing it. You might get home and where will poor Olive be then? Never mind, she will be brave and smile for your good fortune …

It's chaos here in Ward 5 so I must end … How about a romantic ending and Omar Khayyam to the rescue!

> Here with a loaf of bread beneath the bough
> A flask of wine, a book of verse – and thou
> Beside me singing in the wilderness –
> And wilderness is paradise enow.

It filled the page! Seven pages – a record for me!
Love, Olive

Those letters consumed my days and nights. I would spend hours writing epistles of ten, twelve, fourteen pages – and loved every minute of it. Suddenly, life had a focus and a purpose! Just to make this wonderful girl happy. I rewrote *Romeo and Juliet* set in a sanatorium, where we were the principal players; the hospital chaplain, Fr Mulligan, became 'the Friar'; and Sr Moran was 'the Nurse' who thwarted our best efforts on 'the balcony' (hospital veranda). Olive loved it and pleaded for 'more, more, more'. She would regularly conclude her letters with a verse from Omar Khayyam –

> Ah love, could thou and I with fate conspire
> To grasp this sorry scheme of things entire,
> Would not we shatter it to bits – and then
> Remould it nearer to the Heart's desire.

I was growing bolder. I was wondering about life, post Blanchardstown...

You fade away into 'nothingness'?? Impossible – once known, never forgotten! The idea of you fading away into obscurity is too ridiculous to be even considered. How could I possibly forget you? My stay in Blanchardstown has been made so much more pleasant since your entry into my world. What more could I possibly say? Reassured? Good! (What is he saying under his breath?)

What more to say? Your vision at the window this morning – nice! Talk rather limited though – felt very hurt that you refused my invitation to come walking! Terry is much improved since she received a message from you. I think I will have to do something to get thought of 'every minute'!

Your epistles get better and better. More and more and more please – soon, soon, soon!

Love Olive

We were definitely tuned to the same wavelength, although she was the more sensible one, recognising that we were in a vulnerable position, enclosed in an unreal world. When she wrote, *'you are a special person; pity we didn't meet in another time, another place'*, she was being realistic, but it depressed me. On reflection, I feel we would *never* have met in another time, another place.

We were an odd couple, really. She was very outgoing, a 'people person', who loved to socialise and was much travelled. I was shy, somewhat reclusive, dedicated to work and study – a nerd, in modern parlance, I suppose. Yet we resonated off each other so well. Olive certainly opened me out, encouraged my writing talents, took me totally out of myself. Our meeting in the Blanch was meant to be – I am certain of that.

The days, weeks, dragged by. When would I get on Grade 4?

Monday, 9th May – late, late p.m.

Most disappointed – no wave from you on the way home from the pictures. Poor Olive on last legs (how many have I got?) with my sad tale of woe to explain the non-arrival of mail. Reception cool. Sympathy nil. Ned just didn't believe my story (that I had a nasty fall this morning) – and so with great personal risk I sit up and write. Notice tears mixed with ink? Seriously though, I will have to admit I am a total dead loss (got that in before you could!) – falling by the wayside in your time of dire need. Do you think you might have it in your heart to forgive me? You will? Ah – relief, relief! Where was I when the lights went out? With you – how could I forget! Really, I would get first prize for drivel any day …

Someone, somewhere is thinking of you. You are not alone. Everything is going to be alright – it's just got to be! Please, please let me have the news (of your x-ray) as soon as possible – by other means than you suggest!

Love Olive x

P.S. Like being spoiled – you must do it again!

My wardmate, Andy Penston, brightened life up with his humour and sense of fun. He brightened it further by executing a daring raid on Unit 4 and photographing the glamorous blonde in Ward 5. I now had a portrait to drool over! Life was further brightened by the arrival in Unit 2 of a most attractive and caring night nurse, Ann McGarry, who would subsequently become a lifelong friend of Olive and myself. Ann was a breath of fresh air. Never one to be bound by regulations, she would regularly make soup at midnight for the young blades of Ward 5. It was such a change to be treated as adults. I remember saying at Ann's wedding, years later, that I would forever associate her with celery soup – and I do. Ann also encouraged my romance, claiming that Olive was smitten too and 'madly keen'.

Unit 4,
Sunday,

Dear John,
How could you possibly doubt my delight in receiving your missives? When I think of all my efforts (sweat and toil!) in telling you so – and now to hear it was a wasted labour ... Words fail me! I give up, retire from the scene of battle, etc., etc.

Coming Events of Note! In two weeks time, John will be on 'grade' and in eight weeks time Olive goes home – all said with fingers and toes crossed! I wonder what effect 'grade' will have on you (am I treading on dangerous ground here?) I know it has made me feel restless. The first six months here have passed in a haze of make-believe, the outside world fading away into nothingness. Now that the end is in sight, I find my thoughts wandering to things beyond the bounds of my confinement. What about you? Has your sojourn here made any difference to you as a person? Goodness, I'm going all serious – apologies – won't let it happen again.

Radio Requests – I am utterly disgusted with them! Each week I spend a lot of my precious time in thinking up some line of wit for you and all to no avail. My genius remains undiscovered – most frustrating! The only ray of sunshine last week was 'Umbrella Man's' request. Message received – over and out. I have decided not to disillusion Mary over your so romantic request of last Tuesday. Thought it would be unfair as I had already made her the recipient of a black eye!

Incidentally, you will be meeting her on Tuesday – that is, if I don't succeed in keeping her chained!!

What next? Ah yes – your ambiguous comments passed in French. Now, John, don't you realise I am only a simple country girl and cannot be expected to understand all this crosstalk of yours! 'Strings to one's bow,' etc. – whatever is he talking about???

My brief glimpse and short conversation with you this morning has excited me too much to write any more! Must fill the page – what more can I say – nothing – pity – the more dashes the better! Well you played a mean trick on me – sending me an empty envelope on April 1st!!

From 'We're just good friends' – your idea!

Love Olive

P.S. Olive loves (wait for it – no jumping to conclusions!) receiving letters from John.

What an enthralling letter! She really was a rogue. My diary entry for that day recorded a new hope.

A 'missive' from Olive. As I read the opening lines the radio poured out 'Just Friends' ... ominous! A very clever and funny letter. The girl has got what it takes. It gave me a big charge. From what I gather, all is not lost – yet! Will have to read and re-read it! Thanks Olive – good to know somebody cares. Disrupted all my study plans for the night! Later on the radio – 'I'm in the Mood for Love'. Enough!

Finally, on 11th May, 1966, came the long-awaited good news. Dr Holmes put me on Grade 4 and said I could go home in three months! Halleluia! Freedom to roam the wilds of Blanchardstown! Freedom to meet Olive – at Mass, at the movies, at bingo!

The very first meeting came the following evening, when I sat beside her at bingo. We both agreed that the bingo was a nuisance but, otherwise, it was a wonderful evening. I walked her home, to a chorus of catcalls and slagging from Unit 6. Did I care? Not a whit. Every second in Olive's company was precious and too short. Sunday afforded another opportunity to meet after Mass. My diary entry for that day says it all:

Olive suggested the itinerary – down by the hospital, up by Units 7, 12, 10 – through the woods and 'home' by Unit 6. Wonderful, wonderful – still too short. She's a terrific girl – loved just being with her, talking, laughing. Is it mutual? I hope so. This could well be it – I hope so! Thanks, thanks, thanks. Olive – you're a pet!

And then Monday night was cinema night. Life could hardly get better! The movies were not exactly screen classics:
Norman Wisdom in *The Bulldog Breed*.
William Holden in *Father was a Bachelor*.
Tyrone Power in *The Eddie Duchin Story*.

But what did that matter? It was an opportunity to be together – except when an unknowing older patient insisted on sitting between us. The Tyrone Power film gave rise to a particular term of endearment. 'Poochens' was Olive's term. I converted it (*à la* Cockney slang) to 'Eddie Duchins', as in 'I love you, Eddie Duchins' *[P.S. Still do, more than ever]*. The most wonderful movie night of all, though, was the night there was no movie. Again, my diary tells it best:

Monday, 30th May, 1966
Heavenly weather. Lucky for the 'normals' outside who can enjoy it! We knew there would be no film tonight, but no one actually told us that ... So, Pat and I dressed up and hit the road. Olive and Terry from Unit 4 did the same. Being the grand evening it was, we went for a walk – Olive and I leading, Pat and Terry lagging behind. Down to the mortuary – exotic or what! Who passes us in his car but Dr Holmes! Good night! Well, we might as well make a night of it – so, over the gate and through the woods! An absolute panic – over and under fences, through briars, me beating a path, Olive in her high heels. The laughter must have been heard all over the place.

Several wrong turnings later, we emerged at the Boiler House – the summit of exotica! Olive and I walked round and round the Boiler House lawn – sixteen times, according to Terry – and had a great conversation. It was magic! At eight o'clock we had to part. Pat and I returned to base. Sister was livid. She had been looking everywhere for us. 'In future, don't go to the pictures until I tell you!' Nurse Callaghan warned us that trouble was coming – Sister was reporting us to Dr Holmes (Hee! Hee! She doesn't have to!)

I couldn't care less. I had a ball. We may have broken the rules – stupid rules – but have no regrets. As Olive said – some day we'll look back and laugh at this. Reminds me of a line from Virgil:

> *Haec olim meminisse iuvabit – one day it will delight us to remember these things.*

It was a defining evening for Olive too.

I'm lost in a maze of mixed-up thoughts and feelings. Firstly (one must begin someplace!) at the start of our correspondence I never for a second thought things could be as they are. How are they? I don't know and hate having to attempt to analyse the whys and wherefores of our friendship. Am afraid something will be lost in the process. For myself, in a gradual way, our meetings and receiving your letters, etc. (we're back to 'etc.' again!) have come to mean quite something to me.

Sorry to hear via Terry you had to endure a lecture on your return from the woods. Feel a bit guilty since it was my suggestion in the first place. I know I would not have missed it for anything. The situation was so ridiculous. I could have curled up with laughter – all right, I did! Thank you for the request. Yes, my head is still spinning – how about yours?

Had the embarrassment of having to face Dr Holmes on my own in the office yesterday morning. He didn't say anything but had a very knowing smile on his face which put me off completely. Didn't ask him half of what I wanted to …

Until the next time,
love, Olive xxx

P.S. Fr Mulligan was told about our venture. He was most amused and came up yesterday to find out if the 'operation' was successful!

Olive had indeed plenty to ask Dr Holmes. A week earlier, the bombshell had dropped. Instead of going home in a few weeks, she was being sent for surgery. Why this happened, I still don't know. All I know is that I felt shattered for Olive. She must have been devastated, but never showed it. She remained in good spirits, and spoke of the upcoming surgery as if it were a visit to the dentist. If anything, the news drew me closer to her. I wrote longer and longer letters. I wanted to comfort her, be a support to her. I was growing increasingly restless and frustrated, especially after the 'taste of living' in our adventure in the woods. I was totally besotted with this beautiful woman who, to me, was 'full of the milk of human kindness'. I couldn't believe my luck – that she should be interested in me! I would do anything for her – despite an edict that came down from Matron, telling of her concern about 'patients mingling'. My reaction at the time was, 'Why don't they send us all to Unit 8 *[the children's unit]*?'

Olive was moved to the hospital in preparation for her operation – which meant our meetings were fewer. I remember a surreal day – Thursday, 9th June. Olive had to undergo a bronchoscopy – I thought of, prayed for and wrote to her all day long. It was the feast of Corpus Christi, and there was to be a procession through the sanatorium grounds, for which purpose loud-speakers had been set up on the procession route. However, it teemed rain all day, and the procession was cancelled. Somehow, the loudspeakers were connected to the radio, and we had the wonderfully surreal sound of an Acker Bilk concert echoing all over the grounds through the incessant rain! It caught my own mood perfectly.

Our final 'outing' was the day before Olive's operation. We went for a walk to the Boiler House (now known as Inspiration Point) and had a frank discussion on our respective feelings. Olive was so full of warmth and understanding – we would definitely meet in 'another time, another place'. Fate would intervene first, however.

5

Leaving Blanchardstown

On the day of Olive's operation, I received the news that my father had suffered a stroke and was seriously ill. Following a hastily arranged medical conference, I was allowed home (a month before the allotted time) on compassionate grounds. So, on 24th June, I left Blanchardstown, after a confinement of 215 days. They were very precious days to me. I had discovered myself and I had found the love of my life. Ten days later, my father died. I grieved for him greatly. He was a good, honest, upright man. I was also greatly concerned for Olive. I wanted to be with her, but could not. It later transpired that she almost died when she began to haemorrhage after the operation. I only learned subsequently that she had the entire lung removed – a particularly barbarous operation in those days – but she came through it all in true fighting style and, when I did eventually get to visit her, she looked – as ever – a million dollars.

Even in her extreme pain, she managed to write to me.

July 1966,
Hospital 3,
J.C.M.H.,

Dear John,
I am terribly sorry to hear your very sad news. Words are inadequate to convey how I feel for you at such a time. It's so much easier to comfort children – you can pick them up, hug them, dry their tears and to a certain extent ease their pain. It's a pity we're not all children at times.

I know you will be able to accept God's will – however hard. You have such a wonderful character. I pray for your father, R.I.P., for you and your family.

Take care of yourself.
God bless.
Love, Olive x

The visits continued over the summer until Olive was eventually discharged in September. She had been in Blanchardstown for a year. In the same week, I resumed teaching. The letters continued too. I wrote almost daily for the next two years. It was October before we had our first date outside Blanchardstown. I drove to Stackallen, full of apprehension at the thought of meeting Olive's parents – needlessly, of course. I think her father initially looked on me as one of Olive's 'lost causes'. Her family teased her as being the 'Patron of Lost Causes', such was her concern for the down-and-outs and misfits who crossed her path. She railed against injustice and spoke out against it, often to the embarrassment of her family. I must have been particularly nervous that evening, as Olive's father later told me he considered me a 'one hundred to one shot, who came from nowhere on the rails'. Olive had no shortage of suitors. I was just another one and certainly did not impress her father that October evening. The date itself was a near disaster. We drove to Howth, which was enveloped in a peasouper fog. It wasn't the end, thankfully, but the beginning of a beautiful courtship.

Such was the severity of Olive's operation, she had been advised to spend two years in recuperation. Fate again intervened, as it had in my case. A few months into that recuperation, Olive's mother suffered a stroke and needed constant care. Olive's role changed from being nursed to being a nurse. Her sisters helped out, of course, within their own work patterns, but Olive was often on her own with a very difficult patient. It scarred Olive psychologically, ruining her sleep pattern for the rest of her life. Her sisters Maeve and Joan would take over at weekends, thus freeing Olive to come up to Dublin with me. They were wonderful weekends of togetherness and deepening love. How I hated leaving her back to Stackallen on Sunday evenings!

Harmonstown House,
Stackallen,
Thursday, 9th November, 1967,

My dearest John,
Thank you so much for your letters (received two of them today) and Mass Bouquet. Words could not express how much they mean to me and how much they have helped me over the last few days. But, without any letters, just the thought of you is enough to keep me going at any time. Darling, I love you so very much and I count the blessings of our mutual love every day. I know I am not expressing my feelings as I would wish but also know you will understand – thank God!

Mother is in a much happier state. She has become very quiet and very weak. Maeve and I take turns at staying with her. Today I managed to get out in the air for a while. It was lovely to walk through the fields and think of you ...

Will spoil myself and phone you now! Please don't feel you have to write. I know you are thinking of me and that is the main thing. Re the weekend – I'm hoping to make Dublin but won't know until Friday. Longing to see you then.

Please take care.
All my love,
Olive x

In August 1967, Olive managed to get away for a week-long break. I took her to Oughterard, Co. Galway, where we stayed with my sister Kay and her husband, Dick Cotter. We explored Connemara each day, and so began Olive's love affair with the West of Ireland. That Friday, we drove across magnificent wild countryside to the quaintly named Loughnafooey (I have since been told it means 'the lake of the winnowing winds'). The view was breathtaking. Olive was, typically, concerned for a howling dog which was locked out of a cottage down below us. We kissed. I looked into her beautiful green eyes and asked her the question that seemed so obvious: 'Will you marry me?' Without a moment's hesitation, she said, 'Yes.' There had been no plan. It just happened spontaneously. I was deliriously happy – delirious to the point of seeing three beautiful eyes in her face for the next hour! It was a perfect evening. We had come a long, long way from that first swab-test meeting.

Waterford,
October 1967,

My dearest John,
Our sojourn in Waterford is proving most enjoyable and Daddy is thrilled with himself. He is attending two Masses every day, has joined the Third Order and has bought a booklet with the title 'How to escape Purgatory'! Needless to comment, I am having a marvellous time teasing him – no hope for me, I'm afraid!

Your letter has just arrived and has made me all excited and all sad too. Me misses you terribly and loves you so much. What a complaint but how I enjoy it – particularly when we are together … Not to worry, 'Christmas is coming' (I hope!) and the goose is getting fat, etc. Have a horrible feeling I shouldn't have said that – I can just imagine some of your comments! Darling, you bring out the worst in me!

When we arrive home on Wednesday I will have to take care of Mother straight away, so it may not be possible for us to meet. She is bound to be excited, so the presence of another person would not help her. Hope you can make out what I'm trying to say – if you can, you are a marvel! All things considered, it would be better to leave our reunion until Saturday. It seems years away and I feel so lost without you – perhaps you might phone on Wednesday – it would be something to keep one going until Saturday.

Apologies for this dreadful effort. At the best of times, I am hopeless with the pen and at the moment I am not even properly awake! Need your kiss to wake me up! Hope you can make sense of all this jumble. Will make sure you understand one thing – me loves you. Take care.

All my love,
Olive x

Olive's mother died a month before we became officially engaged in December 1967. I remember having to borrow money from my sister to buy the engagement ring. We may have been rich in love, but money was scarce! As a teacher, I was earning about £1,000 a year. We had no home planned, but we decided to begin married life in the West of Ireland.

In July 1968, Olive 'escaped' to Wales for a brief holiday with her brother Jack and his wife, Pam.

My darling Olive,
I'm almost afraid to write this because it might turn out depressing if I keep on telling you how lonely I am – but I must write because I so desperately want to be with you …

I'm sitting in the garden. They tell me it's a beautiful day – sun shining, birds singing, etc. – but for me, no! I live under a big cloud (my mother says I have all the appearances of it!). Oh darling, I'm absolutely and utterly LOST without you – no duck was ever so much out of water! Inwardly I feel so happy for you that you have finally got away from it all and are having a well-deserved rest – but words, however numerous or profound, could never convey my loneliness or love for you at this moment.

When you left on the boat on Saturday, I distinctly felt a few heart-strings go! I stood watching for a half-hour till my eyes strained and I could see no more. All the time I talked to you, kept telling you I love you, prayed for you. Madness? No, just that special way of feeling. Pauline was here yesterday and read Mother's teacup, seeing a wedding and a christening – whereupon Mother looked at me and said, 'My God, has she gone to Wales to have it?' Isn't it terrible what they think of my pet??

I dreamt about you last night – you were back in my arms and it was mmm! – nice! So you see I'm with you all the time, pet, even in my sleeping hours. Oh for the time when I can sleep by your side. Won't it just be heaven to be married, to come home to you, to be able to relax with you and at the end of the day to be by your side, hold you and be so happy, content – and proud to have marvellous you as my wife. Oh my darling, how I long to hold you so close to me again and see those big dreamy eyes full of love, that cute nose, to feel the moistness of your lips on mine, the warmth of your breath on my ear, to whisper the same old words again and again, to feel the tenderness of your finger-tips, to enjoy the sheer thrill of being close to you …

Take care of yourself, my darling. I keep praying for you that every-thing may be perfect for you and that you may have the happiest and most relaxing of holidays. Someday we'll smile at how broken-hearted we were for a fortnight apart! But right now it isn't funny – I am pining away, seriously. But my whole goal in life is your happiness and if you are happy I will gladly pine away.

Thinking of you all the time. Me loves you, me is lost without you. Wales doesn't know how lucky it is!

All my love,
John x

Wales,
July 1968,

My dearest John,
Thank you, darling, for your three beautiful letters. I read and re-read them to give me comfort in your physical absence.

I awake with thoughts of you in the morning and sleep with thoughts of you at night (that sounds a bit dodgy!). You travel with me all through the day and talk with me about all the things I see and feel. Yet, my darling, I'm lonely and wish you were here with me in person. Talk about wanting everything on the same plate!!

Today is beautiful and I am sitting out in the sun writing this letter. The surroundings here are all you and I would ever ask for. You would love it here – mountains all around with sheep grazing on them and a stream running by the house. It is just awful that you are not here to share all this with me. Pam and Jack are so good to me. We are taking a picnic to the sea shortly – hence the usual rushed ending to this missive! Anyhow it's all your fault – I keep dreaming about you instead of putting my dreams on paper. It's a case of 'if I thought less I could write more'!

My darling, I love you so much that anything outside this love is a vague and nebulous thing. My love for you colours all my world so all things are beautiful. Will be home by boat on the 13th – the thought of seeing you on the quay has made me feel all excited! Must away – me loves and misses you very much.

All my love,
Olive x

On Wednesday, 18th September, 1968, we were married in Trim, Co. Meath, where Olive's uncle was parish priest. The ring I slipped on Olive's finger bore the inscription *haec olim meminisse iuvabit*, the Virgil quotation that had come to mind on the day of our 'daring' walk in the woods of Blanchardstown. At the wedding reception, I sang the song 'Try to

Remember' with the lines 'when you were a tender and callow fellow'. Indeed I was, but I was also the luckiest and proudest fellow. This beautiful, beautiful woman, this vision in a black leather coat, had just promised all of her love and all of her life to me.

True to form, I had written a letter to Olive, to be opened on her wedding morning...

My darling Olive,

I know you won't have the time or the powers of concentration to read mail on your wedding morning, but maybe you will spare a minute for a faithful correspondent of the last two-and-a-half years!

The only reason I write is to give you a little giggle, to ease the tension, to make you happy. Come to think of it, that's the only reason I ever had for writing – and, in fact, the reason why I want you to accompany me down the aisle this morning. I'd look a right eejit on my own, wouldn't I? (P.S. You will turn up, won't you??)

As you read this, everything will probably seem in chaos, but a few hours will prove how worthwhile it all was. I know everything will be perfect, pet, so not to worry. I know more than anyone else how much you have done – all practically on your own – and how much you've gone through and I admire and love you madly for it. So these last few hours – this storm before the calm! – must not upset you. I'm with you every moment and I'm going to be the proudest man there is to take you from your father after those forty-three paces up the aisle (I've counted them!).

This is your day, my darling. Sail through it with all the radiance that only you can show. This is the day we dreamed of – let us live that dream. Me loves you, my beautiful one. Me awaits you to make you my wife, to make you happy, happier than you know from here on. This is a historic missive – my last to you in our single state! We've come a long way, pet, but from here on the way is pleasant and paved with love. Come to me, my darling. Come.

John xxx

6

Into the West (1)

After all the traumas of the preceding two years (the Blanchardstown experience, Olive's operation, each of us losing a parent), we decided it would be good to escape to the West of Ireland for a while. I took a position as a secondary teacher in Benada Abbey, a co-educational school with an orphanage attached, in the heart of the Sligo countryside, run by the Irish Sisters of Charity. We rented a cottage on the shore of Louth Talt – an idyllic honeymoon setting!

The first year of marriage was wonderful, of course – we were free to be ourselves at last – but it brought its own difficulties, as it must for all couples. Adjusting from the single life to a life of sharing takes time. On top of that, teaching at second level was a new experience for me and it required a lot of preparation. I was also expected to be involved in extracurricular activities such as football coaching, inter-school debates and the compilation of the school magazine. If that were not enough, I was persuaded to join the local dramatic group. My brief acting career extended to playing the role of Tuppenny Hayes in the Aclare Dramatic

Society's production of M J Molloy's *Daughter from Over the Water*.

Olive was concerned for her widowed father and made a number of trips home to look after him. The year was further disrupted by a two-week strike by secondary teachers. Despite the fractured nature of our first year, we enjoyed our time in Sligo, and were made feel welcome by our neighbours and fellow-teachers. We took a particular interest in the twenty or so orphans (all girls) who had a difficult life, with little on offer to brighten their days in Benada. On a memorable spring afternoon, Olive had a large group of them for tea in our little cottage. They were such loveable youngsters, craving affection and attention. They were so excited to have an afternoon of free-dom, gabbing away, wolfing down the sandwiches and cake, and smuggling women's magazines under their jumpers back to the orphanage.

It was an enjoyable year, but two events in the spring of 1969 brought a decision to return to Co. Meath. I was offered a position in St Patrick's Classical School in Navan. Taking that position would enable Olive to be near her father, and be spared the long trips up and down from Sligo. As it happened, she was in no position to be making those trips. She was pregnant. So, at the end of the school year, we bade farewell to Benada and set off for Navan with a small truckload of our still few possessions. I spent the summer correcting Intermediate Certificate English examination papers (a soul-destroying job) and supervising in the Gaeltacht school in Gibbstown – all in an effort to boost my meagre teacher's salary. With the help of an understanding bank manager and Olive's father as guarantor, we purchased a site and built a four-bedroomed bungalow a mile outside Navan – for what seemed the exorbitant price of just under £5,000.

While I was in Gibbstown, Olive stayed with her sister, Barbara, in Portlaoise.

Portlaoise,
Tuesday, 8th July, 1969,

My dear John,
Thank you for the precious missive. Our enforced separation is very hard to bear at times but dwelling on it only makes things worse. We

will just have to take each day as it comes. Remember the motto on my wedding ring! Also we will have a wonderful time making up for our absence from each other – won't we?

My stay here is progressing along the lines that you would think most suitable! I am going to bed at a reasonable hour and I take Mark for a daily walk. My quality of sleep is mixed but could be worse. My nightly scratch is sorely missed – so are 'other things'! What is she talking about? Despite these drawbacks I am managing to enjoy myself in a quiet fashion. Barbara and I chatter away ad lib to each other.

I don't envy you your job with the boys from Dublin – I imagine they could be very entertaining! Don't forget to see Fr Walsh about the job in St Patrick's – and about the flat. Aren't I mean issuing orders to my poor overworked husband? 'Tis a hard wife you have landed yourself with!

Apart from my fainting episode at Mass last Sunday, 'it' is behaving itself very well, thank God. As promised, I have no intention of going to Mass this coming Sunday. You will have to do all the praying for me.

Please write whenever you have a spare moment. Remember to take your tonic and have as few late nights as possible. Me loves you – madly!

All my love,
Olive x

And on 4th October, 1969, our happiness was multiplied by the arrival of Elizabeth Emer Quinn – whom we would know and love as Lisa. When I visited Olive that day in the Lourdes Hospital, Drogheda, she was positively glowing in the radiance of motherhood. I was so proud of her. And her first question to me? 'When can we have another one?'

I came home from the hospital and – of course! – immediately wrote to Olive.

October 1969,

Lonelyville, Navan!
Sunday night,

My darling,
Seeing as how I won't be with you tomorrow, I must drop you a few lines which you will have on Tuesday morning, D.V.

It was beautiful having that short time together this evening, when I could release some of the feelings welling up inside me. Long for your homecoming, when the floodgates will really open!

Me is so proud of you, loves you beyond words, beyond any human power of description. So why try? If I didn't try, I would crack up altogether. And, of course, you would have to go and look a million and a half times more beautiful! You have no mercy on me at all! Result – I am totally immersed in you and Lisa. Love you, love you, breathe you, dream you. You are my whole life, the meaning and purpose of my existence – especially now when you have given me this wonderful gift, this treasure of treasures, this little soul for God.

Thank you, my darling, for everything – for Lisa, for being so wonderful about everything. Thank you, my God, for her. You knew what you were doing! Help me to be worthy of her. Rest and sleep, my beautiful one. I'll be with you very soon.

All my love,
John x

7

Goodbye, Mr Chips!

The arrival of a baby brings further adjustment to a couple's life – the baby simply takes over! Lisa took a few months to settle and, initially, had a lot of digestion problems. At the time, it was trying and seemed to be never-ending, but we coped.

Adjustment was needed in school also. Teaching in an urban boys-only school was very different to a rural co-educational scene. I seem to remember a particularly lively class of first years, among whom was a cocky twelve-year-old called Colm O'Rourke who, many years later, would become my football hero! I remember an English class when we were discussing Spoonerisms and having fun with boys' names – Tony Booth became Bony Tooth, for example. I am almost certain it was O'Rourke who languidly raised his long arm and suggested – 'Sir, what about Seán White?' End of Spoonerisms! Nearly the end of young O'Rourke!

My teaching career ended in 1970 when I was approached by the educational publishers, CJ Fallon Ltd, and was offered the position of General Editor. I was attracted by the nature of the job but, even more so, by the salary offered – £2,000 per annum (incredibly, almost twice my salary as a teacher) and eventually a company car. It was too good an offer to refuse. It would mean commuting daily to Dublin – common now, but not so in 1970 – and thus a long day for Olive with a very young baby, but she coped well. Olive always coped. The job change helped ease our financial problems, but money was always tight. We hadn't much of a social life. All through our married life, it was a matter of regret to me that I could not offer Olive a better life financially. We always seemed to be scraping by. It wasn't that she expected or demanded better – quite the contrary – but I just felt she deserved better, and I would have loved to have been able to provide that 'better'. In hindsight, others could have provided better, but they wouldn't have loved her as much. What I could and did do for her was to ease her work burden and care for the children (something I enjoyed doing). That was the deal, anyway. In the courting days, in the flush of young love, I had promised to 'spoil' her, so why not spoil her in the most practical ways?

Thirty-one years later, broken by her absence, I would resume writing to Olive…

Otterbrook,
Galway,
11.43 p.m.,
Thursday, 26th July, 2001,

My darling,
There's nothing else for it but to start writing to you again after a 33-year break! Pardon the long delay … Re-reading your wonderfully witty, clever and loving letters of 35 years ago, I am just totally, madly, crazily in love with you all over again. (You rogue! – I had forgotten how well – and often – you wrote.) I love you. I love you. I love you, my beautiful one. I feel exactly as I did when I first read those letters of ours so long ago. Am I being a hypocrite? Am I just clinging to the past? No. No. A thousand times no. I want to believe and do believe this is all your doing. In the background Johnny Mathis is singing:

'What'll I do with just a photograph
To tell my troubles to?'

What'll I do, indeed? I need you so desperately. Please stay with me. Don't ever leave me again. Please protect me. Please. Please. Please. I just want to know that you're happy and you're here! There too – wherever, whatever that is.

I'm madly preparing for your party, because that's what you wanted, and that's what you shall have. Poor John Joe Quinn came in earlier with a Mass card and stayed for a coffee and at least five cigarettes. 'Ah Jeez, she was awful fond of this place.' And they were awful fond of you.

By the way, I love you. Did I mention that? Your photos are on display all over the place, I know you'll be mortified, but I want everyone to see them, and talk about you, and say how beautiful you were. This time 25 years ago, you were in the throes of labour, giving birth to our beautiful son. Thank you for him. He misses you greatly too. Please help him.

Your letters are a wonderful source of consolation to me. They recapture that time so well – innocence, discovery, tenderness, unfolding love. Read one today where you gave me instructions on how to get to your home in Stackallen. My first visit! I was so nervous. No wonder your father considered me a 'hundred-to-one' shot. I think he thought I was one of your 'lost causes' ... The letter is postmarked 4/10/1966. Exactly three years later you would give birth to Lisa. Were we fast movers, or what?

Johnny Mathis is now singing 'My one and only love'. You were. You were. You were and you are, and you will be, my one and only love. It was a beautiful, beautiful love story, and nothing can ever change that. We went off the rails, or ran on different tracks latterly, and I so much regret that now. Please forgive me for all my stupidity, and please stay with me now, and always. Need you so badly. Love you. Love you. Love you. Stay. Please, please stay. Be all about me. Miss you so terribly.

All my love,
J x

More spoiling was needed in May 1972 with the arrival of Deirdre Quinn. To give birth to two children, and to care for them with the limitation of one lung, was no easy feat for Olive, but she managed it and managed to grow more beautiful in doing it. All of this, despite lifelong problems with sleep deprivation and, of course, when you have an invisible handicap like a missing lung, you often get little in the way of sympathy and understanding. Occasionally I would be guilty in this respect myself. *[You shouldn't have looked so beautiful, love.]*

Despite her isolation with two small children, Olive managed to forge a social life of her own, through liaison with other young mothers in the area. She took up golf for a while, and became involved in politics, acting as secretary to the Fine Gael *cumann*. (Politics was in her blood – her father was a first cousin of the former Taoiseach, John A Costello.) She loved the cut and thrust of local politics, and would come home from meetings to regale me with stories of the antics of local councillors. World politics would also impinge on our lives, however, The oil crisis of the mid-1970s sent petrol prices rocketing and, suddenly, commuting to Dublin became very expensive, even with the experiment of car-pooling. Reluctantly, we began to contemplate leaving Navan. Circumstances in my employment soon made that move a reality.

2.35 a.m.,
Sunday, 29th July, 2001,
In bed – exhausted!

My darling,
The young ones are still partying below, but the rest of us have collapsed! O my darling, what a day! Did you enjoy it? Let me know – please. A wonderful, bittersweet day. Beautiful Mass. Aiveen and her singers carried out all your wishes – 'Amazing Grace', 'Ag Críost an Síol', 'Like the Deer', 'Be Not Afraid' – I did the reading, and spoke about your love for Killeenaran. It was more difficult than at the Funeral Mass, but I got through. Then down to Bernie's pub for 'a drink for Olive'. Back to prepare for the party. The food! All your women friends

came up trumps again. You would – correction, did – love it. I know. I sang 'Try to Remember' – our wedding-day song – for my lost bride, and we toasted the Champagne Lady with Cava. The singing was great, but poor Mary O'Toole just couldn't sing – she was too emotional about you. I gave it my best shot for you, poochens. I love you so very much. That's all I can repeat, like a mantra.

Listening to Shirley Bassey singing 'What are you doing the rest of your life?' Me too. What am I to do for the rest of my life, but cling to you? I love you so very much. Totally exhausted. Totally in love with you. Night-night.

Guz Guz x
John x

8

A Career in Broadcasting

At the end of January 1975, the hammer-blow landed. Fallon's informed me that they were terminating my employment. I was, in their view, not commercially oriented enough. As far as I was concerned, I had given my all to the best of my ability – overseeing the publication of as many as thirty new titles a year. I had to be master of all trades and subjects, from Leaving Certificate Technical Drawing to reading schemes for primary schools. That was the nub of the problem. I was stretched in too many directions. But I was proud of my work overall, and I had enjoyed my five years in publishing. If the Unfair Dismissals Act had been in force then, I would have taken Fallon's on, but I had no such avenue open to me. I was given a month's notice. No golden handshake. No handshake.

It took a while for reality to sink in. Here I was, with a wife, two young children and a mortgage – and I was unemployed, and without a car. I was so numbed by the experience that, on the day I handed back my company car, I made a phone call to my (very) understanding bank manager, and went straight out to buy a new car! I held my head high. I was proud of my work. But I was unemployed! A return to teaching was a possibility, but it might take time. Olive was, as ever, a rock of common-sense support. I had the feeling that something would turn up. And it did.

While serving out my notice, I noticed an advertisement for the position of Education Officer with RTÉ, part of a team behind a pilot schools radio service. Experience in education desirable. I applied, was called for interview and re-called for a second interview. An agonising wait followed during the month of March – when I really was jobless – until eventually the letter of appointment arrived. We could breathe easily again.

Looking back, the Fallon's experience was a valuable part of my education. They may have deemed me a 'failure', but I never accepted that. And neither did Olive. It was part of life's experience and I was ready to move on to a new and different world.

Bray,
1.40 a.m.,
Wednesday, 1st August, 2001,

My darling,
Here I am – back again! I know I'm 'back again' – I mean back again in Bray! Via work, for which I had zero enthusiasm … Hated leaving the house. A tearful car-journey – dangerous for driving! Your photo beside me on the way.

Awake last night from 3.30. Finally made a 'tup of tea' and sat up reading the Blanchardstown Diary. Our first meeting on Easter Sunday 1966. So green (me!), so innocent, so tender, so beautiful (you!). It was a beautiful love story. The letters confirm it. And now … Now I'm racked with guilt. The last ten years. Coldness. Pride. Fucking stupidity. Ann Henning's poem haunts me:

My love, when you die –
If you die before me –
I shall grieve...
oh how I shall grieve

for each moment of our life together
that we had and did not treasure:
precious gifts left unopened,
blossoms trampled underfoot.
Celebrations
lost forever.
Sacrificed.
Waylaid.
Oh my love, how I shall mourn them.

Forgive me please. And be all about me. I'm so totally confused about the 'hereafter'. Doubts set in. What if – as you used to tease Derry – there were none? You must stay close to me, pet. If you don't, I'll just crumble. Feel so empty. Drained. Tired. To sleep, perchance to dream. How lovely it would be to dream of you. Night-night. Guz-guz. Me loves you.

John x

9

Into the West (2)

I joined RTÉ as an Education Officer on 7th April, 1975. *Radio Scoile*, a ten-week schools radio project, was being piloted in primary schools in the Gaeltacht areas. I was assigned to the Connemara Gaeltacht to evaluate the programmes as they were broadcast, observe the children's reactions and the teachers' use of the programmes, talk with teachers and children and feed this evaluation back to the programme-makers in Montrose. Because of the length of the project, we decided to move *en famille* to the West for the duration. We rented a house in Oranmore. Little did we think that, sixteen years later, we would move permanently to another house eight miles down the road.

The work was interesting, and involved visiting schools all over Connemara and in the Erris peninsula in Mayo. Locating some of these schools, mostly one- or two-teacher schools, was a task in itself, but it was a joy to see the possibility that radio could offer children, particularly when they were in the care of an imaginative and enthusiastic teacher – sadly, not always the case. As for the Quinn family, they settled in very well in Oranmore. Lisa went to the primary school that was literally across the road. I remember a swarm of local children attending Deirdre's third birthday party, even though we were only a month in the place. And the weather was exceptionally good. It was a happy time. Olive and I enjoyed a good social life and, when we returned to Navan at the end of June, we brought happy memories with us.

Commuting from Navan to Donnybrook (even in the 1970s) became increasingly problematic in terms of cost and time, and we reluctantly decided to put our first home on the market and move nearer to Dublin. We spent the spring and early summer of 1976 house-hunting, something which became a race against time, as Olive was pregnant again. In June, we finally decided on a three-bedroom bungalow with a large garden in Greystones, Co. Wicklow, and a month later, on 27th July, Declan John Quinn was born. Our family and our happiness were complete. (Regarding the former, I recently came across a birthday card from about that time which Olive had signed 'Love from Olive, Lisa, Deirdre and Declan. FULL STOP!) In August we moved house, always a traumatic event, leaving good friends and neighbours. In Olive's case, it was more difficult as, once again, she was moving away from the father she adored.

We had been blessed with three beautiful children. I was so proud of Olive with the way she coped with each birth and with the subsequent development of each child, given that she only had one lung. The years dim the memory, and it is only now, when I see Lisa coping with her baby, that I realise that once we had three children under seven, with all the attendant problems of illness, schooling, etc., and I say to Olive in daily chats with her: 'We were bloody brilliant!' And it was *we*. Even though this was before the advent of the 'New Man', I participated fully in the children's care and development, from nappy-changing to visits to the doctor. Seems (and should be) normal and natural now, but then it wasn't. I did it because I enjoyed it and because it was one of my ways of helping Olive through, one of my ways of loving her. I was always a practical lover! Olive didn't drive in those days, so I ferried her most places.

While the foundation of our marriage was solid, our relationship took the roller-coaster ride that I suspect most couples experience. Money – or the lack of it – seemed to be a perennial problem. Doctor's bills and med-ication were constantly eroding any spare spending power we had. I always claimed I was entitled to shares in the local pharmacy, such was my con-tribution to its upkeep! As a result, our social life was diminished. I was never a pub person and, while we did get out for the occasional meal, Olive felt – justifiably – that she was deprived. She was very much a people person, and her main social outlets then were outings with female friends. It rankled with me then that I couldn't give her a better social life; it rankles even more in hindsight.

Things were not improved by events at work. The *Radio Scoile* pilot was deemed a success, but there was no government funding forthcoming for its expansion. The three education officers were maintained with research projects on various educational radio and television programmes. RTÉ encouraged me to pursue an MA in Education in University College Dublin, in order to extend my research skills. The MA was done by thesis and exam. It was the thesis part that nearly caused my undoing and a pos-sible divorce! I decided to study children's leisure pursuits and was per-suaded by a friend in the research business to do this by the 'diary method' – i.e. 1,000 children around the country would complete diaries (blocked out in half-hours) on how they spent their leisure time on a particular Tuesday, Thursday and Sunday in June 1977. Simple! Simple? Try reading 3,000 diaries and coding them for a computer under twenty different pursuit categories! I spent weeks – day and night – half-demented by this exercise. Olive was not amused! One of the few bonuses for her was that I could take a break from coding to give Declan his night-time feed!

Of all those diary entries, one stands out – a boy who simply wrote that his entire afternoon was taken up with 'firing stones'. Given that the stones were not aimed at a local glasshouse, I thought, 'What a wonderfully productive afternoon!' What dilemmas he must have been wrestling with! What solutions he must have (hopefully) come up with! I often cite this instance for the value of 'doing nothing' (as many of his peers wrote). But he and his peers did nothing for my marriage! I did get my MA and the friend who suggested the 'diary method' is still my friend. My future would not be in research, however. From the first day I walked into the

Radio Centre in RTÉ, I knew what I wanted to do for the rest of my career. I wanted to be creating and making radio programmes.

Under a bough – à la your beloved Rubaiyat! – overlooking 'my field' in RTÉ, 4.46 p.m.,
Wednesday, 1st August, 2001,

My darling,
They call it 'my field' because I protested when it was converted to a car park. This year it has been returned to its field state! Fields … I read a 1967 letter of yours this morning where you said that all the respite you needed from caring for your mother was to get out in the air – 'It was lovely to walk through the fields and think of you' …

That touched me to the deep heart's core. Here I am, 34 years later, desperately looking for respite from my grief, getting out in the air, walking this field, thinking of you … Clutching my little photo-album. Snatching glances from times past …

I love you so much, my beautiful one. So very, very much. That's all I can say. All I need to say. And all I need to know is that you are here with me 'beneath the bough'. Rest your head on my shoulder. Give a little sigh of contentment. Love me. Lean on me. Never, never, never let me go.

John x

Photo Album

Babes in the Wood – Olive with her twin sisters Barbara and Clare.

Do I have to do this?

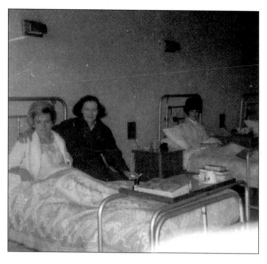

'The glamorous blonde in Ward 5.' (See page 44.)

'Down to the mortuary – exotic or what!' (See page 47.)

Wedding day, 1968.

The Black Leather Coat – in Greece.

Our first home, Lough Talt, Sligo.

With Lisa in Navan.

Politics in the blood. With John A Costello and his cousins, Olive's father and uncle, as Costello was given the Freedom of Dublin in 1975.

All of us there, Greystones 1981.

At the launch of Must Try Harder. *(See page 115.)*

What Lois remembers. (See page 122.)

The Open Mind Guest Lecture 1998, University College Cork, with Senator George Mitchell and Helen Shaw, Director of Radio.

At the Jacobs Awards 1988.

10

Making Radio

The opportunity to fulfil my dream came when Tom McArdle, one of the three original *Radio Scoile* producers, moved to television. I applied for the vacant radio producer position and was successful. It was the most important career move of my life. I knew I would love the job, and that's how it turned out. To be paid to do what I loved doing was a pleasant bonus. Ironically, Olive had doubts about my taking the job. She felt I would not be able for the criticism that would attend it! I was happy to prove her wrong in this instance.

Even more ironically, it was all her doing anyway! I have always felt that, if I had never met Olive, my life and career would have plodded on safely and predictably. I would have remained a reasonably good teacher, would possibly have been promoted to the position of principal, and would now be retiring from teaching not a little frustrated, cynical and tired! An okay life. But because I had met this beautiful, unusual and gifted woman, had fallen totally in love with her, and because she had seen in me the person she wanted to share her love and her life with, I walked through life with an inner confidence and belief in myself that would ultimately release the creativity I have enjoyed in my broadcasting and writing careers. It wasn't a case of her ever urging and driving me on (though she always said I should write – she *knew* I could write winning letters!), it was just the fact that I had won her heart that made me feel I could take up challenges other than teaching, and find my true niche. It may seem simplistic, but I know in my heart it is true. That is why I said to her in the radio programme *A Letter to Olive* (belatedly, I admit), '*You made me the person I am. My real date of birth was 1st March 1966. Throat-swab test. Vision in a black leather coat. Door closed in her face. Do I make myself clear?*' It was the power of love and, of course, my regret is that I did not make myself clearer during our life together.

12.25 a.m.,
Friday, 3rd August, 2001,

My darling,
And still the letters come … One from Chris Burke. Remember him? He remembers us being the first people to invite him to our home when he joined the teaching staff in St Patrick's in Navan. And a very touching letter from Colm O'Rourke whom I taught as a cheeky 12-year-old in St Patrick's and who went on to be my football idol …

And now the doubts come. Strange, weird, frightening feeling tonight that you had 'wandered off' – your presence had 'evaporated'. Don't want this to happen. Read the Blanchardstown Diary, your scented letter, etc., but still had that feeling. Sat in the dark, listened to music, pleaded with you. I know you'll laugh but in my irrational, immature (what's new?) way, I wondered if you had met up with someone new! I can hear you laughing, but I'm in the depths. Feel alone. Cold. You can't have left me just like that. Is it your way (someone's way?) of telling me to pull back, 'get out of the past' rut, move on, as they say? Feel I failed you in so many ways over the last ten years. Should I leave these letters, stop writing those poems? No! Wrote a little poem called 'Trivia' today that pleases me, warms me.

Where are you, my beautiful one? Please come back into my space. Please. In desperation I have put on a 1988 radio interview you did about Open Door ... Of course it seems as if you're here in the flesh – never went away. Unreal. (P.S. You were brilliant in the interview.) But it does draw you near – and it has cheered me up.

Before I go to bed – another card from my cousin Mary Frances. She quotes John O'Donohue – 'Grief is a journey that knows its way. Though travel is slow through that grief-journey, you will move through its grey valley and come out again into the meadow, where light, colour and promise await to embrace you.'

Will you be there to embrace me? And where are you now, my beautiful one? I want to love you. I want you. I need you. Hopefully a new day will bring you.

Guz x Guz x
John

TRIVIA

Let us talk of trivia –
Inconsequential
Insignificant
Half-remembered things.
What the children did
And said;
Characters we met,
The antics of a much-loved pet;
Our secret language
'The K is B ...' (kettle's boiling!)
'I'd love a tup of tea ...'
Nothing events
Like the note I left –
'I leaned against
The washing machine

And set it going ...'
You laughed so much.
Like I said
Silly, inconsequential
Trivial things –
Things that bound us
Together,
Impenetrably ...

I began life as a producer with *Radio Scoile*, which was still limping along with a limited service for secondary schools. I remember being totally in awe of Niall Tóibín as he read Frank O'Connor's story 'First Confession' for a Junior English series. I had actually *produced* Niall Tóibín in my very first programme in my new role. Later that year (1977), I took over Tom McArdle's series *Knock at the Door* – a charming little programme which offered songs, rhymes, stories and things to do for the very young listener.

The very week I took it over was clouded for Olive and myself. Her father – the man who claimed I was a 'one hundred to one shot' in the courtship stakes (and he was right) – died at his home in Stackallen. A part of both our lives had ended but, for Olive, the loss was enormous, such was the love she had for 'Bert'.

11

Radio Days and Holidays

My career in radio gathered pace as I grew in confidence and experience with the medium. The great thing about working in the Education Department (as it was then) was that, under its head, Maev Conway-Piskorski (whose father had taught me in primary school), you were given *time* to work on projects. Unlike the treadmill of current-affairs programmes and chat shows, education programmes were subject to careful planning and piloting, and I think it showed in the finished products. The range of subjects was quite broad, and if you had an interest or expertise in a particular area, you were encouraged to exploit it. Over the next few years, I moved from a children's magazine programme, *Alphabet* (whatever happened to children's radio?), through *I Remember, I Remember* (series of interviews on childhood) to two important series for parents – *Learning to Read* (how parents can help the pre-reading child) and *Children Reading* (a parents' guide to children's leisure reading). The first interview I ever did was the pilot for *I Remember, I Remember*. My guest was Seán MacBride, and I listened with fascination as he recalled, in his beguiling French accent, how, as a boy, he flew kites with W B Yeats on a Normandy beach, or was treated to stories and ice-cream in a Parisian tea-shop by the writer James Stephens. This was *work*?

I was bursting with ideas for radio. It consumed my working life. Olive always claimed I was a workaholic. I always rejected that, on two counts. Firstly, I detest the word as it is not a word, but an example of the bastardisation of a beautiful language. Secondly, I disagreed, even in the accepted sense that she intended. I have never let my work dominate my life, or interfere with my duties as husband or father. I didn't bring my work home with me as workaholics are often charged. Yes, ideas came to me during my home life – how I might structure this programme, approach that series, etc. As a radio producer, you are in the ideas business, and they came to me (thankfully) often unbidden and spontaneously, but they never became the addiction of workaholism (to use another non-word!). I simply loved my work, loved the challenges and possibilities it offered. In that sense, it wasn't work at all, more a hobby. I wasn't into other hobbies like golf or 'going out with the lads'. My other hobbies were simply home and family life and, because of the nature of my work, I could, and did, often work from home and structure my working day in ways that helped Olive. I was there to give her mornings off, bring the children to school, etc.

The rewards for all this love of work were simply the satisfaction of having made something worthwhile and the response of listeners. Occasionally, they went further than that. In 1981, I won the prestigious Governor of Tokyo Award at the Japan Prize (a major international competition for radio). It was for *The Miracle Tree* – a programme on language development in the young child. Whatever occasional friction there might have been about my 'workaholism', no one was more delighted with my success, or more proud of me, than Olive, and we celebrated in style. Other awards would follow over the years.

11.45 p.m.,
Saturday, 4th August, 2001,

My darling,
This morning, at an ungodly hour, you woke me with

> 'Long ago and far away, I dreamed a dream one day
> And now that dream is here beside me ...'

I sang that to you in our courting days, so you organise my waking to it now, don't you, pet? This is your way, isn't it? Your way of 'staying with me'. I want to stay with you, be with you. This may sound horrible in one way, but I really feel I have nothing else worthwhile to do here. The children could do without me, although I know they will say otherwise. Workwise, I've done all I wanted to do. Honestly, I would prefer to leave and be with you. I really, really would.

I spent the afternoon watching football on television, but this photograph beside me is haunting me. I only found it recently. Where has it been all these years? Who took it? In some park? Before my time! You are so, so beautiful in it. I can't take my eyes off you and I can't bear to look at you! You are so beautiful. I have cried my way through two football matches – nothing to do with the football! – just repeating the mantra. I love you so very, very much. I cannot tell you often enough. It is beautiful and it is heartbreaking. My beautiful one. My one and only one. [This is the photograph used on the cover of this book.]

I know you are in touch with me through this photograph. It's that look in those beautiful eyes. I love you. I love you. I love you. Want to be with you. Only you. You know that now. You must know it. I am so desperate. I need to talk this out with someone. I just love you so much. Can't take my eyes off that beautiful face. Stay with me. Haunt me – remember how you used to joke that if you went first, you would haunt me! Haunt me now, I beg you. I love you so very much.

*What am I to do? What am I to do? I want to be with you – now
and forever. I just love you so very, very much.*

Guz x Guz x
John x

In that same year of 1981, we began our love affair with Rosslare. For six
successive years, we rented a house there for the month of July. The only
way we could afford this was to rent out our home in Greystones for the
same period. There would be a big tidy-up at the end of June (why does
your home never look better than when you are renting it out to complete
strangers?). Then, on 1st July, we all squashed into the car with the dog,
the two budgies, the tennis rackets, the sun-chairs (relics of the Papal visit)
and the clothes, and the clothes. I know too well how Noah felt in the Ark,
as we set off on that two-hour drive. (No, we are *not* going back for your
favourite doll in the whole world!) They were very happy times – a wonderful closeness as a family, invariably good weather, freedom for the children
– especially when we rented a little chalet which they dubbed 'The Little
House on the Prairie' – and a special closeness for Olive and myself. No
work ever intervened – well, just once when, in 1985, I had to come back to
Greystones to interview Charles Handy for four hours on the future of work.
It was the beginning of a long and fruitful friendship, and a dinner in Kelly's
Hotel won Olive over all too readily.

What an irony that we would spend the last day of our holiday together
in that hotel, and that Olive would die swimming in those same waters that
we had frolicked in. An irony? I think not. I like to think that, if she had the
choice, Olive would have opted for the time, place and circumstances of her
departure from this earth – happy, swimming in the Rosslare sea on a June
evening while staying in Kelly's Strand Hotel.

11.30 p.m.,
Sunday, 5th August, 2001,

My darling,
Here is the news.
1.   *I love you so much. (That's news?)*

2.   *Meath 2–12, Westmeath 3–9. They got out of jail again! Declan*
      and I aged several years in Croke Park, but we squeezed out a
      draw. You certainly would not have been able to watch it and
      would have been 'all a tingle', as you wrote many years ago.

3.   *I love you so very much.*

4.   *Declan is off the cigarettes and has rented a computer. I knew*
      you'd like to hear that, but then you probably organised it!

5.   *I love you so very, very much ...*

And your photo continues to haunt me – beautifully! I talk to you in
the tenderest and most loving ways – like I did in the courting days
(how quaint that expression seems today!) Why couldn't I talk to you
like that in latter years? Don't know. I regret that I didn't make a bet-
ter effort. Stupid. So stupid. Anyway, now it's like a damburst. The
love and the tears flow – regularly. And you are here – I know that.

God, you were so beautiful! I really wasn't worthy of you. I thank you
for becoming my wife and partner and again I crave your forgiveness
for any hurt I caused you. I love you so very much. Am I boring you?
I just love you – and it's beautiful – achingly, achingly beautiful.

Love,
John x

12

Sunshine and Happiness

Olive's health became an increasing concern throughout the 1980s. In the spring of 1981, she was hospitalised with a lung infection that followed a bad flu – a very serious illness for someone with just one lung. A holiday in the sun was recommended. We scraped the money together and she went off to the Algarve in March with her sister Joan. I didn't go, because we couldn't afford it, the children were still at school and, anyway, I am not a sun person. It gave me time to reflect. I kept an occasional diary in those days and, on St Patrick's Day 1981, I wrote:

I really miss Olive, for all we differ and clash and irritate. There is no one like her and I love her – so.

'There is no one like her!' How those words scream out at me now! Sometimes it takes an enforced absence to make you see the obvious! Of course we argued, and had differing opinions and, at times, irritated the hell out of one another. But deep down, there was no one like her. That is what attracted me to her in the first place. That is what caused me to fall in love with her – her values, her gentleness, her kindness, her concern for others and, of course, her stunning beauty which for me only reflected the beauty within. An enforced absence of two weeks brought me to my senses then. An enforced absence of however many years rifles it into my brain now. There is, was and will be no one like her for me. Get that into your head, you silly man, and be glad you had her presence, however fraught at times, for thirty-three years.

Olive came back from the Algarve that March looking a million dollars and feeling a million dollars. If only we had a fraction of a million dollars to send her there every year! We didn't, but we scraped together enough, somehow, to send her to the sun for the next twelve years or so. Mostly to the Algarve, sometimes to Spain, usually in the autumn to boost her strength for the winter. Two weeks – sometimes three, if there were bargains going – usually with a girlfriend, but on a number of occasions on her own. I know family and work colleagues often raised an eyebrow at the latter, and probably thought dark thoughts, but we were just being practical and *trustful*. I had already used up my annual holidays, the children were back at school and, anyway, we simply could not afford to go away together. So Olive enjoyed the sun and I enjoyed my work. We were not being madly liberal at all. I wanted Olive to be strong and healthy and therefore happy and, on those grounds, the sun holiday worked. We weren't *that* kind of couple at all. *[Were we, dear?]* Come to think of it, that's all I ever wanted for Olive – to be happy. I know I had funny ways of showing it at times, but that was the goal. Beginning and end of story.

Diary of a Lost Soul

[Excerpts from a 1983 diary kept while Olive was on holiday in Portugal, recovering from illness]

Day 1:   *Well we waved to you as you took off. (Did you see us?)
I can't remember having tears in my eyes saying goodbye
to you going on holiday before ... Brought the children to
see E.T. (more tears!) and then to Granny's for tea ... Just*

*now I pray you're sleeping, ready to wake to healing sun
and air. And I miss you. And I love you.*
*P.S. As I was washing the dishes in Granny's I thought of the
mop you brought to apply suntan oil to your back ...*
P.P.S. Who's the mopper?

Day 3:   *Cold and wintry. So am I. I see you're 'fair and hot'! Did you
need the mop yet? I think of you a lot – and say a little
prayer. Night! Night!*

Day 4:   *Bin day! Joy of joys! Still cold and showery. John Kennedy
of JWT tells me the weather in the Algarve is fabulous.
Hope you're enjoying every second of it. The mop? I wonder
who's mopping her now ... Lisa made beautiful lemon custard
tarts. Deirdre (age 10) made trouble ...*

Day 5:   *Got official confirmation of Senior Producer Grade today.
You certainly picked the right week to go away – winter is
still here. And all I've got is a hot-water bottle. And all
you've got is a mop! That's what worries me ...*

Day 8:   *I hope you didn't try to ring us as Lisa was tricking with
the phone – ringing the talking clock. Result – the line is
jammed and every time we lift the phone we get – 'At the
signal ...' Drive you round the bend. Had difficulty persuading
Deirdre to go to Mass today (Sunday). She 'doesn't understand' Mass and finds it boring ... I was particularly lonely
for you today. Don't know why – just thought you might
like to know. Think about that while you're being mopped ...*

Day 9:   *Hooray! The talking clock is gone! Boo! The rain is back! I
see you were only 'Fair and 64°' – hope you're not depressed
too. No post from Portugal yet ... I'll have to post this today.*

Guz x Guz x. Be good – and if you can't, be careful who you give the mop to! Miss you. Love you. Please get better. And strong. And madly passionate. Come home and devour me!

Love,
John x

The trouble with happiness and its pursuit is that life keeps getting in the way. We hope for the best. We hopefully try our best, but the vicissitudes of life conspire to frustrate and thwart us. In our Blanchardstown days, Olive would write witty 'postmarks' on the envelopes of her letters. I remember one of them which summed up Olive's frustrations – 'No postman! Now rain! Life!!'

These simple frustrations would be writ large in our married life. Of course there were happy times, very happy times – the photograph album is as good a book of evidence as any – but life, married life, is really about coping with the down days, the 'typical ould Mondays' (to quote James Plunkett) when things go wrong, the boring days when nothing much happens, the 'deep freeze' days when opinions don't so much differ as clash violently, the moody days, the days of illness, the days of hurt, the days you would want to forget. Every relationship has them, but doesn't always admit to them. All you can do is try to get through them, around them, over them. Sometimes you succeed, sometimes you don't try hard enough, sometimes you just run away.

Now, of course, I can see those 'down days' in true perspective, and so many of them were so ridiculously trite, and we were both so silly not to see them as such, but *then* they were so big, so insurmountable. We humans are a strange, strange species! And, of course, hindsight brings regrets, big-time regrets. A stupid, stupid occupation, I know, but who doesn't fall foul of it now and again? I am comforted by a neighbour in Galway in this regard. 'I have no time for this regret stuff,' she says. 'If you didn't travel the road you travelled, you wouldn't be where you are now!' Very Irish, but very true! It is the path you take in life that makes you the person you are. Given my total and complete love for Olive *now*, the road we took was worth all the potholes and wrong turnings. *[I just hope you feel the same, love. Someday we'll sort it all out! In the meantime, I am sorry for all the times I didn't try – and yes, dear, I know I could be trying at times!]*

11.15 p.m.,
Monday, 6th August, 2001,

My darling,
Just back from a live radio production of The Tempest. *Brilliant! 'Chaos becomes order through magic, forgiveness and love.' I'll drink to that!*

Prior to that I went to see Mary Magee. What a wise and inspirational woman at 92! In five words she unlocked my troubled mind – 'Heaven is nearer than Galway'. She went on – 'Olive is with you now all the time, loving you, all-knowing. You are closer now to each other than ever.' It is so. I know it. Feel it. She was such a consolation.

As was Anam Chara *when I read it this morning. 'Pascal says, "In difficult times you should always keep something beautiful in your heart." Perhaps, as a poet said, it is beauty that will save us in the end.' Indeed. And beauty is truth … And in our case, the something beautiful is you, my love, and our beautiful gentle, tender love. Of that I am convinced, my darling.*

If that wasn't enough, we had Lyric FM all day with its 100 most requested pieces of music. Sheer joy! Thank God for Lyric and for music. And you, of course, are the music. Stay very close to me, my beautiful one. As Prospero reminds us:

> 'We are such stuff as dreams are made on
> And our little life is rounded with a sleep.'

Love you always,
John x

13

The Open Door

Sometime late in 1982, Clare Dunphy knocked on our door. Clare was the local public health nurse and she lived just around the corner from us in Greystones. She knocked on the door with a purpose.

In her daily work, Clare was coming across an increasing number of physically disabled adults who were literally prisoners in their own homes. They had no social outlets, no opportunities to develop their talents, to be the people they could be. This wasn't right, Clare thought. To compound matters, the disabled were being cared for day in, day out – and night in, night out – by devoted partners, parents or family members (who, in many instances, had given up their careers to care for the loved one). Equally, the carers were very often prisoners – willing prisoners, but prisoners nonetheless. This certainly wasn't right, Clare thought. The system was failing these people. She voiced her opinions but nobody was listening. 'We need someone who is *political*, someone who will kick up a fuss,' she said to a friend. 'I'll try Olive Quinn!' She obviously knew Olive Quinn better than most, and when Olive opened the door to Clare that day, it was a symbolic beginning to a quite extraordinary adventure.

As a child and as a young woman, Olive was always teased by her family as being the 'Patron of Lost Causes'. If there was a 'lame duck' or a down-and-out in the vicinity, Olive would be the one who would show practical concern for that person – an alcoholic, a Traveller, a homeless person, a beaten wife – 'oh, another of Olive's lost causes', they would say. Scoff they might – and we *all* occasionally scoffed – but Olive had a fierce sense of justice. She simply could not understand, and would not tolerate, injustice in any form, and refused to walk away from it. Of course, *we* could be embarrassed by all of this. 'Look, don't get involved,' *we* would say. 'Not our business. The government's fault. Leave it. You'll get yourself into a mess. And what about your own health?' All the excuses we could muster for our own inadequacy, our guilt. They cut no ice with Olive, and only made her more determined. Once she got her teeth into injustice, she was the proverbial terrier. Would not let go. Oh, she was 'political' all right. Clare Dunphy had chosen well.

The test case that Clare outlined that day concerned Helen Clarke. Helen was the only child of Kevin and Phyl Clarke and, at the age of twenty-one, with a wonderful life before her, she developed a brain tumour which paralysed her and left her with a life of quiet desperation in a wheelchair. Kevin, a recovering alcoholic, had to continue working, to maintain his family. Phyl was frail and arthritic. A desperate situation. Olive went to visit them and the Clarke family subsequently became good friends of ours. More importantly, she was convinced about Clare Dunphy's argument. There were other Helen Clarkes about. A centre was needed to provide care and development for the disabled on a daily basis, and, equally, to give respite to their home-carers. And so the struggle began.

11.20 p.m.,
Tuesday, 7th August, 2001,
(My mother's 99th birthday!)

My darling,
Three most extraordinary things to tell you about. You know already,
but I'm telling you anyway!

1. *Went from work into town on the bus. Declan happened to be on the*
   same bus! We spent the journey going through my mini photo album
   of you. He is such a lovely lad – everyone says it. There is so much of
   you in him. What other 25-year-old would stand there in D'Olier
   Street and kiss his father goodbye?

2. *Decided to walk back to RTÉ for the exercise. (Who's good?) Coming*
   through St Stephen's Green, I remembered a glorious autumn day last
   year when we sat on a bench in the Green and just enjoyed the con-
   tentment of it. In memory of that I sat down for a smoke and was
   actually leafing through the photo album (again!) when I was accosted
   by a down-and-out – one of the three guys who were lying on the grass
   across from me. 'Any chance of an ould cigar, boss?' says he. I gave him
   one, hoping he would go away but instead he sat beside me, lit up and
   told me his story. A former jockey who had ridden for all the big
   names. Threw a few races, was brought before the stewards and lost his
   licence. Everything went downhill from there. Hit the bottle, marriage
   broke up and here he was living rough, on the touch in Stephen's Green.
   He was a really likeable guy – witty and articulate. ('I have no intention
   of leaving this planet just yet.') You would have enjoyed him – one of
   your 'lost causes'. I gave him a few bob and got up to leave. For some
   reason, I told him I had lost you a month or so ago. He embraced me
   (I can hear you laughing!), leaned forward and whispered in my ear:

'The seed in your heart shall blossom …'

Just that. Extraordinary! Weird! Wonderful! He stunned me initially.
When I looked back he gave a little wave and mimed the message
again – 'The seed in your heart shall blossom.' Poetry! Quite beautiful
really. It was you surely? It could only have been you. Thank you.

3. *Later, listening closely to your favourite ABBA song, the words jump out –*
   When the time is right
   I'll cross the stream
   I have a dream
   I believe in angels

   Are you talking to me or what?

   Love,
   John x

The initial response from the health board was disappointingly predictable.
The numbers weren't there to justify a day centre. A handful of people,
they said. Olive joined forces with a friend, Mary Hackett, and with
Pádraigín Hughes, whose husband was disabled. They did their own
research, carried out their own census, travelling the highways and byways
of North Wicklow. The 'handful of people' grew to thirty, forty, maybe
more. The three women made their case and continued to lobby. They
enlisted the support of Monsignor John O'Connell, the dynamic parish priest
of Holy Redeemer Parish in Bray, a parish noted for its range of innovative
social services. He, in turn, enlisted the help of prominent businessmen in the
town who would act as trustees for the project. The wheels were turning.

Olive was in her element now. The politician in her revelled in a challenge. This was not charitable work, in her view. It was simply a matter
of rights, of justice. The physically disabled and their carers had been 'lost
causes', but their patron had arrived, and woe betide the authorities who
took her on! The project needed a name. Olive came up with one. Open
Door. A symbol for inclusiveness, for welcome. The disabled would not
be 'patients' or 'clients'. They would be *members* of a warm, embracing

community. Olive threw her energy and time totally and willingly into Open Door. Her energy was limited, given her health problems, but it was never a disadvantage. She had the time. The children were all at school and, while they now recall Mum being almost constantly on the telephone (we won't talk about the phone bills) when they came home from school, they were always her first concern. And the husband? Well, he was good at writing letters, remember? So he wrote letters (willingly) to ministers, health board personnel, the Wheelchair Association. He wrote letters.

It all came to fruition in December 1984, when agreement was reached and the Open Door Day Centre for the Physically Disabled opened in temporary premises in Fatima House, a Legion of Mary hall in Bray. The beginnings were rudimentary – six members and a staff of three. The members were collected by ambulance and brought to a place where they could socialise, pursue interests and crafts, avail of physiotherapy and occupational therapy, and have a hot meal delivered daily from Loughlinstown Hospital. But from day one, what immediately impressed the visitor was the wonderful atmosphere of warmth, enjoyment and love that permeated the centre. I was so happy for the three women who had worked so hard, but I was immeasurably proud of Olive. She had proved that it *ought* to be done, it *could* be done – and now it *was* done. And Clare Dunphy had a knowing smile on her face …

11.40 p.m.,
Wednesday, 8th August, 2001,

My darling,
Lisa rang from London this morning to tell me that there was a tribute to you in The Irish Times! *Raced down to the newsagents mid-breakfast (only for you would I leave my breakfast!) and there you were – Pat Hunt's glowing appreciation – gloriously in the middle page of* The Times. *I cried with delight and pride. Love you to bits.*
Tim Kennedy from Open Door rang. He can't believe you're gone. You meant so much to him – he 'would follow you to hell and back'. I played my new CD of Tchaikovsky's 'Pathètique' Symphony just to savour

your theme – the slow movement. It has always reminded me of you – elegant, languid, graceful. I read your hospital letter 'postmarked' No Postman – Now Rain – Life! (How I loved those 'postmarks' of yours.) How brilliant you were! How wonderfully – and quickly – we fell in love: 'Nice to know we've tuned in on the same wavelength.'

And you appreciated my King Lear quote:

'No, no, no, no …
We two will live alone
Like birds i' the cage …'

I got as big a thrill reading it today as I did in 1966. I love you so very much. Please stay close to me. Lots of comments on your tribute, including a phone call from an upset Pádraig Mac Gréine, now in his 102nd year.

P.S. I'm upset too. Please come and live in the cage with me.

John x

APPRECIATION

Olive Quinn

The Nobel prize-winner Seamus Heaney paid an exquisite tribute to the late Olive Quinn, who will long be remembered for the key role she played in establishing the Open Door Day Care Centre in Bray.

Speaking at her graveside in Shanganagh cemetery, he picked up on some words of the liturgy of her funeral mass in the Church of the Most Holy Redeemer.

"Heaven," he remarked, "is one of the first words we become aware of in childhood." Seamus observed that as we grow older the idea of heaven flourishes more in our minds than in images formed in childhood. How right he is. With the passing of time the names, images and personalities of loved ones gone to heaven populate and crowd our minds and memories.

Seamus recited his beautiful poem *The Wishing Tree* at Olive's graveside.

In the poem he thinks about his recently deceased mother-in-law. "I thought of her as the wishing tree that died/ And saw it lifted root and branch to heaven." The poem concludes: "I had a vision/ Of an airy branch-head rising through the damp cloud/ Of turned-up faces where the tree had stood."

Olive was a "wishing tree" who fulfilled three great wishes: to love, to be loved, and to make life easier and happier for the physically handicapped and their families. Indeed, the olive tree possesses a wealth of symbolism: peace, fruitfulness, strength, victory and reward. All of these qualities Olive Quinn possessed, and more.

The Open Door Day Care Centre is the enduring manifestation of her love for her fellow human beings. How appropriate it was that three wheelchair-bound members of Open Door brought gifts to the altar before the Offertory of the Mass. Open Door is not just a haven; it is a heaven on earth for its members.

Many people and institutions worked long and hard to create it, but the initial idea was Olive's. In the early 1980s she developed the project with her friends Mary Hackett and Pádraigín Hughes. Father John O'Connell PP arranged to make Fatima Hall available to them in 1984. An army of fundraisers, led by Joe Duggan and Jim Daly, joined the project, and in 1987 the Open Door facility moved to Boghall Road. The Department of Health, Eastern Health Board and the Wheelchair Association also played pivotal roles in its development. In 1994 Open Door moved to its present, purpose-built premises on Vevay Road, where more than 80 members enjoy its benefits.

Olive's commitment to her cause became legendary. During protracted negotiations she could talk entire delegations into submission to her will.

Never robust in health, she could use her delicate disposition to disarm and charm budget-conscious officials.

Olive radiated style, personal and verbal, and had a dress sense that made her appear as royal as her native Co. Meath.

Openness and generosity of spirit are qualities we associate with Olive and her husband John Quinn. It is fitting that she founded Open Door and that John's programme on RTÉ Radio One is called *The Open Mind*.

Olive is in heaven now, no doubt bending the ear of God to make even more good things happen for the members of Open Door. May she enjoy her eternal reward.

The grateful people of North Wicklow extend their condolences and appreciation to John, and to their children, Lisa, Deirdre and Declan.

14

Keeping the Door Open

Opening the door was a difficult enough task. Keeping it open proved in many ways more arduous. The centre operated under the aegis of the Eastern Health Board, but the Open Door trustees were committed to raising a substantial level of funds each year to maintain its operation. Over the years, there followed the succession of initiatives that every voluntary organisation must pursue in the never-ending quest for funds – Lord Mayor campaigns, fashion shows, Christmas Day swims, cheese-and-wine evenings, barbecues, concerts – we had them all. Soon after his first Eurovision win, Johnny Logan succumbed to Olive's charm and agreed to be the official starter to a sponsored bed-push from the GPO to Greystones! It was a particularly difficult time for local fundraising, as global issues, such as the Ethiopian famine, dominated. As well as competing with each other, many deserving local causes were also competing with Live Aid.

I made my own small contribution to Open Door by compiling and publishing a book called *Must Try Harder*, a collection of school memories from sixty well-known personalities. We sold about 5,000 copies at £5 per copy. It was done, as I said in the preface, 'with love and admiration for Olive'.

The centre was recognised as an outstanding success within a couple of years. This was reflected in its winning a Bray Civic Endeavour Award, but success brought its own problems. The growing membership, and the facilities they needed, put increased pressure on Fatima House. New premises were needed. Olive was chairperson of the Board of Trustees and became involved in lengthy negotiations for a health and fitness club that became available on the Boghall Road in Bray. Open Door eventually moved there, but it was never an ideal location, being situated in the middle of an industrial complex. As it happened, Glaxo, the industrial giant next door, needed to expand its premises. The pressure was on Open Door to move again. More negotiations, on top of the quite considerable task of running a growing project, put a strain on the Board of Trustees, and especially on its chairperson. Olive relished the cut-and-thrust of the boardroom, but often became angry and frustrated when difficulties arose, internally or externally. She had a simple dream – that Open Door would be the best day-care centre there was, just because its members were entitled to that. She was perhaps naïve at times, but her commitment to the success and growth of Open Door was total and unflinching. She would often come home from board meetings angry and frustrated that others could not agree with her point of view. She fought many battles. Not everyone saw things her way, but they could only admire her grit.

Midnight,
Thursday, 9th August, 2001,

My darling,
The things one thinks of … When did I first kiss you? Can't remember
– sorry! – but I know it was beautiful and I'm certain I was in love with
you before that.
Anyway – had a nice meal with Declan and Kelly tonight. They're
a pair of dotes. We talked about you lots and I talked to you lots. Love

you lots …Before that I went back for more consolation and wisdom to Mary Magee. The woman is a saint – there are no two ways about it. She talked of God perfecting our relationship. He didn't take you away. He just raised you to a higher plane. 'Olive's 'Purgatory' is her edging closer and closer to God … you only ever wanted her to be happy, so now you must learn to accept that hers is the ultimate happiness. It will be painful – very painful – but she is closer now than ever. There is no physical separation – you in Dublin, she in Galway – anymore. She is with you. She knows.'

It is so. You are 'in the light'. Perpetual light. You know how much I love you. Miss you. Want to be with you. I'm still thinking of that down-and-out. 'The seed in your heart will blossom' … It will be so. Is so. Love you so much, much, much. Forever.

John x

Open Door eventually found its permanent home in October 1994, when a new purpose-built centre was opened by the then Minister for Health, Brendan Howlin TD, on land acquired from the Loreto Sisters on Vevay Road, Bray. It continues to thrive, with a membership of eighty, a wonderfully dedicated staff – both paid and voluntary – and exceptional facilities but, above all, it is permeated by that same atmosphere of warmth and love that filled Fatima House twenty years ago. With no disrespect to all who have worked for and in Open Door, it is Olive Quinn's lasting legacy to North Wicklow. I know I am biased, but I also know exactly how much Olive spent herself in pursuit of her dream. Everybody else saw the elegant and beautiful woman who presided at meetings and official functions, the tough unyielding negotiator, but only I saw the woman who suffered all her married life with sleep deprivation – often driven to the point of feeling almost suicidal. Only I shared with her the depressing prognosis her chest consultant delivered to her in the mid-1980s – her one lung was expanding to fill the vacuum in her chest cavity and, in doing so, was pulling and twisting her bronchial tubes, leaving her liable to repeated infection. Did she ever use these continuous health problems to gain sympathy, or to score a point at board level? Never. Did she ever look anything less than the proverbial 'million dollars' at any function or meeting? Never. I don't know how she did it. She was quite an extraordinary woman. There really was no one like her.

11.45 a.m.,
Saturday, 11th August, 2001,

My darling,
Just sitting here listening to the 'Romeo and Juliet' Overture, gazing at your photo. You are so, so beautiful. The sheer radiance of your face. Is that how you 'look' now? I know that's stupid, but I still like to think so. I love you so terribly much — no arguments, ifs, buts, questions about it. More in love with you than ever. All your fault. Your beautiful fault.

Thought a lot on my way back from my morning walk. Can't believe my luck. How blessed I was that you replied to my first letter (written in German!) and to all the subsequent ones; that you wrote to me two or three times a week (you who hated writing) — often when you were in severe pain after that barbarous operation; that you slowly unfolded your beautiful nature to me; that you met me for our first date and then didn't say — 'well, you're a nice guy, but …'; that you continued to meet me and that we fell in love so beautifully and so rapidly; that you said 'yes' to me 34 years ago tomorrow in Connemara; that you agreed to give your love and your life to me, who was so raw and naïve and immature but so, so, so very much in love with you. For all of that, my darling, I thank you with all my heart. Truly, I wasn't worthy. Truly. No bullshit. No false modesty. Truly.

No wonder I walked on air then! I really did! This is all pouring out of me just like the tears. I loved you. I love you now more than ever. In between? Disgusted with myself over lost opportunities of the last ten years when we seemed to drift apart … I know I can't fix the past but I know I always did things for you. That was my way. Spoil you. Your first letters said how you loved being spoiled. So I spoiled you. Not enough. 'You spoiled her,' they said, making it sound like a crime. Why shouldn't I have spoiled you? That's what it was all about. Why didn't I say that to them? Why didn't I spoil you more? Especially latterly. Why? Why? Why? I know you weren't 'yourself' in the last five years, but why? Why? Why?

Why am I pouring this out? Because I have to. Because I love you so much. This is tearing the guts out of me. I love you. I love you. I love you, my beautiful one, my only one. Thank you. Thank you. Thank you.

John x

On top of all that, Olive suffered severe whiplash injuries in a car crash in 1987. Her health problems seemed never-ending. 'They'll have to shoot me in the end, like they shoot horses,' she used say. But she kept going. And because she always maintained her looks and her dress sense, no one knew what she was really going through. Except me.

I burst with pride whenever I walk through the Open Door Centre now – pride in someone who fought so hard and at considerable personal cost to realise her dream. When Olive died, I wanted to leave some lasting tribute to her in the centre. I found it in a photograph taken in RTÉ in 1985 at the launch by Pat Kenny of *Must Try Harder*. Olive is standing on a chair making her chairperson's speech (a thing she hated doing). I am holding her hand for moral and positional support. People are laughing. It is a wonderful photograph, taken by our friend Ray Flynn. I went back to Ray to have it enlarged. I then had it framed and presented to Open Door. The caption says, 'I Have A Dream' (Olive's favourite ABBA song). Underneath I wrote that I chose the photograph for four reasons:

1. It was taken at an Open Door function.
2. Olive is making people happy – if you ignore Messrs Kenny and Quinn who are seriously perusing *their* speech notes.
3. Olive is head and shoulders above everyone else!
4. I am holding her hand!

Enough said …

Loughnaphooey,
Co. Galway,
4.28 p.m.,
Sunday, 12th August, 2001,

My darling, my darling, my darling,
Here I am 34 years later – almost to the minute – back in Loughnaphooey on a dreary misty afternoon. Here on the most beautiful day of my life, I held you in my arms and asked you the only question I could ask you, 'Will you marry me?' And you said, 'Yes. Yes. Yes.' And I kissed you so tenderly and looked so lovingly on your beautiful, beautiful face. And you had three beautiful eyes – an extra one on your forehead! And I was so unbelievably happy. Unbelievably. And I loved you so indescribably much.

We looked down at a cottage on the riverbank where you were so concerned over the sheepdog who seemed to be locked out or abandoned. And I kissed you again and loved you even more. There was no plan. It was just you and the place and the moment. Never was a question so obvious. Never was an answer so immediate and so certain. Thank you so much, my beautiful darling. No regrets. I only delight in the memory of it all.

Now – the tears flow as freely as the mountain stream cascading down behind me. That photo sits on the steering wheel. You gaze at me, smiling, and you're saying Yes. Yes. Yes. I'm here, you're saying. I'm here, darling, and I love you too. That's what you're saying. Such a beautiful face. Such a beautiful place. My heart could – probably will – burst with joy. Why did we never come back here? Why? There are so many whys. Forget that now. We are here now. So close. So close. Your presence envelops me. And I am so, so happy. So lonely but so happy. So, so much in love with you.

The cottage is derelict now. No dog! The rain sheets across the valley. Your radiance shines through the gloom. Hold me now, my beautiful one. Hold me and keep saying yes, yes, yes. I will give my life and my love to you for all of that life – and beyond. Hold me. Love me. Stay with me. My beautiful three-eyed one. I love you so very, very much. That's all I can say. Want to say. Forever. And ever.

John x

15

Into the West (3)

By the end of the 1980s, Open Door was thriving. Olive loved the house in Greystones and we had good neighbours, but she was growing restless. She felt that Greystones lacked a sense of community. It was fine if you played golf or tennis, but if you weren't the sporting type? There were several voluntary associations (and Olive did have a brief dalliance with Fine Gael again), but somehow she never found the community sense that suited her – not that Open Door left her with much time for any other commitments. Greystones was a fast-expanding dormitory town, but, for some reason, it was not offering her contentment. Maybe her health problems were greater than even I knew; maybe she was just tired and needed new pastures; maybe, most of all, she was just a country girl at heart.

When the country was going bananas over Ireland's exploits in the 1990 World Cup, we were on holiday in Spiddal, Co. Galway. The landscape and the people seemed to re-awaken something in Olive – a longing to be part of that landscape and people whose openness she responded to instantly. Another dream was forming in her head. Could we not live here in the West? I was initially sceptical, but Olive persisted. Of course, it was a romantic idea, but it could be done. I would still have to be based in Dublin, but there were regional studios in Galway and Limerick. I was tempted by the idea. It was not something we could have done when the children were small, particularly given Olive's health problems. Now the girls had flown the nest, and there was only Declan, who had started secondary school. The onus would really be on Olive, who would have to do without me for four or five days a week. Maybe that was a pleasing prospect for her! Who knows?

12.45 a.m.,
Thursday, 16th August, 2001,

My darling,
I begin to the strains of 'When I Fall in Love'. This has been a very difficult day. It began with my going through a diary from the 1970s – it brought home to me how I had failed you. Endless problems with money – debt, debt, debt – rows, no proper social life for you, my occasional 'misbehaviour'. How you had traipsed around with the children – to Navan, to Cork – to give them a holiday. What a miserable life you had then. I really let you down. I am so sorry.

Then to cap it all I came across a letter from the early 1990s about what was a misunderstanding over insurance money. You were so low, so unhappy – 'are there any fences left to mend?' ... I destroyed the letter but it practically destroyed me. I went to Mass in Ballinderreen yesterday in abject and utter despair and regret, begging your forgiveness for all the hurt and what seems very little love. What was I at? What were we at? I am so, so sorry, my pet. Please forgive me. Please. I feel you have every right to just wander off 'out there' and be rid of me, but, please believe me, in my strange way, I did love you – and I do so love you now. I have to believe that you know that now – now that you are 'in the light'. I love you so very, very much. I just want to start all over again.

All my 'achievements' – academic, my books, my radio productions, awards – seem pretty worthless right now. I feel so low, so rotten but so, so much in love with you. Crazed. I am absolutely terrified you will wander off on me. Called in to your bank in Oranmore with your Death Certificate to close your account. Am I really doing this? I asked myself. The last straw …

Drove back to Dublin and then what awaited me? Letters from all over – the news of your death is only spreading now, thanks to Pat Hunt's obituary.

Some examples:
An absolutely beautiful detailed letter from Cardinal Cahal Daly

'I did not have the privilege of knowing Olive but it's clear she was quite a wonderful lady … she is still close to you … and she has only gone as far as God and God is very near.'

I am so proud of you – that a cardinal should be moved to write about you.

Elizabeth Handy
'Although Charles and I never met Olive, I feel I almost know her, as you often spoke of her – and you were obviously a devoted couple.'

Pegg Monahan
'Being without Olive is a hard road to walk – and healing and peace come dropping very slow.'

Edith Newman-Devlin
> '"But true love is a durable fire
> In the mind ever burning
> Never sick, never old, never dead
> From itself never turning."
> (W Raleigh)

What luck – out of all the women you could have met and married, to have chanced on someone with those lovely qualities.'

It's true, so true. The letters go on – I almost burst open there at my desk, reading them. Little Angela Murphy from Presentation Radio who 'couldn't approach me in person' (one of many, I suspect) and who had been 'relentlessly' lighting candles for you.

'Talk each day to Olive and she will help you.'

I do. I do.

Lois Tobin (from the Lady Gregory Society)
'I only met Olive with you at the spreading of Catherine Gregory's ashes at Coole Lake. She was so gracious and I recall you helping her over the steps and her smiling at you.'

Isn't that just beautiful? Such a trivial thing, but remembered.

Doireann Ní Bhriain
'It's a very long time since I met Olive but I have a vivid memory of her energy, dynamism and enthusiasm in her work with Open Door.'

Tom Grealy
'I am just someone who listens to you on the radio … I offer you my sympathy … What I read confirms how very special your wife was.'

Karen, Anne and Sue (your hairdressers)
'We were so shocked, it has taken us till now to write … Olive was such a charming, attractive, witty lady … she could exasperate you but it was only to achieve perfection! … she was so well read and loved to chat … we all miss her so much.'

And so it goes. What a mail to receive in one day! It broke my heart
reading the letters but it lifted me too. I just love Lois Tobin's memory
– it reminds me of your 1967 letter, 'it was lovely to walk through the
fields and think of you'. O my beautiful one, if only I could rewrite
the script ... I know that's stupid but ... I did, did, did love you –
and love you even more now, now that the scales have been lifted from
my eyes and the dam has burst in my heart. Please forgive me. Please,
please, please stay with me. I need you so much. I feel I will break in
two. I only have to look at that photo – Radiance, Radiance,
Radiance. How beautiful you must be now in the 'perpetual light' ...
I couldn't be worthy but I need you so desperately. Snuggle in to me.
Don't wander off. Stay. Stay. Stay. I love you – forever.

John x

It was a colour photograph in the property section of *The Irish Times* that
initially caught our eyes. A two-storey thatched house on the sea in South
Galway – not an area we knew at all. We originally had Barna/Spiddal in
mind. We went to see it – on a scorching, blue-skied June day in 1991, the
sort of day one should *not* view a house, I suspect. Of course, we fell in
love with the place. Who wouldn't, on a summer's day – a most unusual
house at the end of a boreen that led to an inlet of Galway Bay. And yes,
there were roses growing by the door. And the vendors were even throwing
their four hens into the bargain, for God's sake! *The Good Life*. Things
moved at a bewilderingly fast pace after that fateful day. Our own house
went on the market. We put in a bid for Otterbrook (the Galway house).
We waited and juggled and waited, trying to narrow the gap between
what the sale of Sunset (in Greystones) would realise and our top offer for
Otterbrook. We went for it and, by mid-July, the deal was done. The final
piece of the jigsaw fell into place when Olive's sister Derry, who had been
widowed two years earlier, moved to Bray in the same month of July. I
now had a place to stay while working in Dublin.

Myself and Grennan, our Labrador dog, were the advance party when
we moved house on 19th July 1991. The driver of the articulated removal

van, having negotiated the boreen with great difficulty, got out, looked around and said with a sigh: 'Oh, it's a grand place alright – if you could stand the quiet!' A true Dub! And he was right. Killeenaran is a grand place, nestling on an inlet of Galway Bay, with the blue hills of Clare to the south and the mountains of Connemara beyond the lights of Galway City to the north. A magical place, full of wildlife and colour, and rich in heritage. Alongside our boreen alone, there is a 6th-century saint's penitential bed and a *cillín*, a children's graveyard.

For all its beauty, living here would mean a major adjustment in our lives. As I lay down to sleep on that first night, with Grennan at my side for company, I had niggling fears. Over the next twenty-four hours, the fears grew into panic. What had we done? What if this doesn't work? What if the whole thing was a mistake? I rang Olive. 'No,' she reassured me, 'we will be fine.' It was not a mistake. She had a good feeling about the place. Everything would be alright.

The reaction of family and work colleagues ranged from astonishment to admiration. Ye are mad! It cannot work! Well, fair play to ye! A lot of us dream it, but ye went and did it! We would obviously have a bit of convincing to do – of other people and, to be honest, of ourselves. There were major adjustments to be made. We had only one car. Olive would need it (we lived three miles from the nearest supermarket) and so, perforce, she began to drive after an interval of over twenty-five years. I would travel up and down by bus – not a prospect many would relish, but it did not bother me, initially. Declan went to boarding school at first. That did not work out, so he changed to a day school in Oranmore, eight miles away. Transport had to be arranged. A whole new pattern of living emerged, for all of us.

Olive took to country living immediately. She was a country girl for whom life had come full circle. She loved the natural beauty of the place, the relaxed pace of life and, above all, the people. She got to know the farmers who passed the door each day on their way to commonage. She would engage them in conversation and discuss the ills of the world and the parish. What they made of this glamorous woman coming to live in their midst can only be speculated on, but they warmed to her instantly.

And why wouldn't they? Our circle of neighbours and friends grew, particularly with the help of Olive's parties. A memorable one in December 1991 celebrated my fiftieth birthday and the winning of another Japan Prize Radio Competition. Declan presented me with two Ailesbury ducks as a birthday present. Duck-eggs for breakfast! Life was good!

10.45 a.m.,
Friday, 17th August, 2001,

My darling,
To the music of Dvorak's 'New World' Symphony … where would I be without music? It is such a balm. It evokes memories, yes, but it links us in a special way. Thank God for Lyric FM. Had a long chat with Anne O'Neill yesterday. You would (do!) like Anne. She's very grounded, very perceptive. Warned me not to be crucifying myself and told me to hold on to this beautiful love I have for you. Bet your life!

This morning I read from Sr Stan's book, Now is the Time, *on death – prompted by Anne who recalled Stan telling me on air that 'Heaven is just a few inches above the tallest man'. Stan talks a lot about 'letting go'. If we let go of painful experiences, we can be transformed, we can grow. Letting go means living with the greyness and foggy insecurity of life. We must trust this 'land of don't know', because it is from here that wisdom comes forth. Living with 'don't know' is letting go. It means waiting, accepting the not knowing.*

Yes, I accept that, but I need help to do so. Please help me, Lord. Please help me, my love. 'Don't know', according to Stan, is open to miracles and insights. I need insights, love. Help me. Help me to grow. What I'm not letting go is my beautiful love for you (our beautiful love?). I love you so very, very much. This is my beautiful unbidden mantra. So easy to say … The dam burst. Such a comfort.

It's not clinging to the past. It's not trying to 'fix' the past. It's the now – the beautiful now and the promise of the even more beautiful future – an eternity. I'll wait, my darling. I'll accept the 'don't know' but, in the meantime, I will love you so very, very much. 'All I Ask of

You' from Phantom of the Opera *has become my theme song. I play it over and over.*

> No more talk of darkness
> Forget those wide-eyed fears
> I'm here, nothing can harm you
> My words will warm and charm you
>
> Let me be your freedom
> Let daylight dry your tears
> I'm here with you, beside you
> To guard you and to guide you

Please let it be so, my darling.

John x

16

Parallel Tracks

Life was good – and creative – in the early-1990s. Before we moved west, I had begun writing fiction – something Olive had always encouraged. My first book, a children's novel entitled *The Summer of Lily and Esme*, was very well received, and won the Bisto Children's Book of the Year Award in 1992. Two more children's books followed before I launched into my magnum opus, an adult novel set in border country, covering a span of some sixty years. It was called *Generations of the Moon*, and it took me three years to write. It sold reasonably well, but I felt it should have done much better. I was, and am, very proud of it.

On the broadcasting front, *The Open Mind* began in 1989 and would run for thirteen years. It was a straightforward – mostly interview – programme, featuring interesting people and ideas, and it built up a committed audience over the years. I have been genuinely touched by the loyalty and affection of listeners. I will always remember the Cork woman who wrote, 'I never went past primary school, but you have been my third-level education.' I have always looked on myself as a conduit in bringing ideas to a wide audience, and have been privileged and fortunate to do so. I became involved in documentary-making – easily the most challenging and rewarding radio work – and made several educational and summer series. A series of important interviews, *My Education*, was published in book form in 1997 and, again, was very well received. Life was indeed good. Professional life.

On the home front, our relationship was becoming strained. As the Galway years went by, Olive and I seemed to be travelling on parallel tracks – but at least in the same direction. Olive was extremely happy in Galway, even though family and friends wondered how she could endure the winters, particularly, on her own for most of the week. For someone who was so outgoing and sociable, it was certainly a challenge, but she made her own life and was content. In my case, the weekend was too short. Five hours travelling in either direction shortened it even more, and my time in Otterbrook was largely taken up with the practicalities of life, such as maintaining the house and garden, helping with housework and preparing firewood for the week. We seemed to have less and less time together, although we managed a social life of sorts – a concert in Galway, meals out, parties, etc. It was an uneven time, however. The travelling was eventually getting to me, and four-hour bus trips became more a nightmare than a novelty. The lifestyle was eating into our relationship.

At the other end in Bray, Derry, Olive's sister, was becoming more and more dependent on me. She developed emphysema, and her health deteriorated quite rapidly from the mid-1990s onwards. I was stretched at both ends.

From the mid-1990s, Olive's health also became a serious problem. She began to suffer blackouts and developed blood-clotting problems. She was put on Warfarin tablets. Her speech became affected at times. She would know what she wanted to say, but sometimes 'the words would not come'. Equally, her writing gave indication that something was wrong. The writing itself became 'spidery' and she would have trouble with simple spelling and the order of words. Her personality seemed to change too. At times, she became irrational and unreasonable, the latter being something I would never have associated with her. I was genuinely worried for her. I pleaded with her to consider moving – at least to where she would be nearer the services she needed (we lived ten miles from her GP, pharmacy, etc.).

What use could I be, 150 miles away, if she had a blackout and fell on the stone floor? She wouldn't hear of leaving Otterbrook. It was where she had found happiness. I had my job; she had Otterbrook. She agreed to get a panic alarm button, and she was surrounded by good neighbours. This was true but, in most cases, these were neighbours who had young families and their own busy lives to lead. Olive was adamant and, when Olive was adamant, that was the end of the argument. She was happy in Otterbrook. I knew that, but it was happiness at a price. With hindsight, I know I could and should have handled the situation better at times. I know I hurt her and was not always understanding of her plight, but the situation was growing more and more impractical. Derry's health deteriorated further. She became a prisoner in her apartment and, consequently, more and more dependent on me, to the extent that I had to spend some weekends in Bray.

9.55 p.m.,
Sunday, 19th August, 2001,

My darling, my darling, my darling,
I am so, so lost! Never imagined it could be as bad as this. I'm sure you're laughing now! Please don't. I'm hurting so much. Love you so much it hurts. It's beautiful but it hurts. Love you so very much. That's it. Nothing else matters. I need you so much. Need a sign that you're here.
Watched Galway hurlers beat Kilkenny – they'll be dancing in Bernie's pub in Ballinderreen tonight! – and just cried my way through it. Not for Kilkenny – for you! And the evening was so long. Afraid of getting into a rut – you must help me. Be calm. Accept the not know-ing … But Jesus, I love you so much – when the sunlight fell on that photo this evening, it was indescribable. The sheer radiance, the absolute beauty. How did I ever win you? Thank you, thank you, thank you, my one and only love. I couldn't look at you any longer – too, too much.
Yesterday it rained – and rained – and rained! Went to Greystones to see Olga last night. As ever, she produced the champagne in your memory. She knows Loughnaphooey well and says it means Lake of the Winnowing Winds … Nice! She also reminded me that she had asked

*me in recent years if I still loved you and my reply was in the affir-
mative. Actually what I said was 'Unfortunately yes!' Sorry about the
'unfortunately'. I could never, would never, have left you. There was
always that tie there. It was called Love. Pity I didn't show it better
but … All that is wiped now. Has to be. I love you still, now, always
and forever. Today I rang Gillian Deeny. She was a great help as ever.
Reassured me that you loved me and were so proud of me.*

*So here I am. Drained. All cried out. Fondling your ring which
is a great comfort. Longing for you. So lost. So lonely. Help me, pet.
I must be patient. I must be calm. I love you so very, very, very much.*

Guz x Guz x

A part of my reaction to all of this was to accept its inevitability, and plunge
myself more and more into my work. (I almost became a workaholic!) I
would work late in the Radio Centre five nights a week. My programme
output increased, but it was an unnatural and, ultimately, unhealthy lifestyle.
The only real winners were RTÉ and the listeners who would enjoy my
output. In 1999, I was diagnosed as having prostate cancer, and underwent
a prostatectomy. Olive came up to Dublin while I was in hospital, and
was so attentive and caring then, and subsequently during my convalescence
in Galway. It proved, if proof were needed (and maybe it was) that, despite
all our problems, deep down there was a solid foundation to our relationship. It was proved again two years later, when Olive became seriously
ill. It was a foundation of love. We argued, we differed, we lived in different worlds at times, but we loved each other, despite all. Life!

The 'Galway Experiment' worked for Olive, but, to be honest, it did
not work for me. We had good times there, we made good friends, but
the distance from work and the travelling ultimately put too much of a
strain on our relationship. At the end of the day (literally), we all like to
come *home* from work. Eventually Fate took a hand.

12.30 a.m.,
Tuesday, 21st August, 2001,

My darling,
Have just turned off a disgustingly violent film on television. Why I watched it till then I don't know. That's one of the 2,379,643 reasons I need you here ...

Anyway, the big news! At 2.23 p.m. yesterday our little 'Lee-Lou' gave birth to an 8lb baby girl. Everything went well – that's all the detail I have. What could I do but cry – for you. Just by eight weeks you missed it ... I know you were there, but you know what I mean. O my love, I hope she has some of your genes and much of your beauty. It's a strange feeling being a granddad – I just want to share it with you. I am so happy for Lisa and John, but, but, but ... You, my darling, you, you, you. Where are you, my pet? I hope John is even a fraction as proud as I was when you gave birth to Lisa. I remember I bought you an antique rocking chair! And when I first visited you in Lourdes Hospital, you asked me, 'When can we have another one?'

Bought a gold chain for your ring. The jeweller did say he could split it and enlarge it to fit my finger, but no! I couldn't do that. So now you nestle close to my heart – and it's a good feeling. Ray Conniff is playing 'Dancing in the Dark' – how I wish it could be so, my love. Love you, love you, love you. Someday we'll dance in the light. Someday. Eight weeks. Eight long weeks. Clare says it will take five years. What will take five years? For me to 'get over it'? I will never rest until we meet again. Never.

But we have a grandchild. The line continues. And I'm glad it is a girl. I knew a girl once. She was so beautiful that I married her. Don't know what she saw in me but I adored her. Still do. Still do. Stay with me forever, my beautiful one. Forever young. Forever my beautiful love.

John x

12.17 a.m.,
Wednesday, 22nd August, 2001,

My darling,
Today I heard our grand-daughter cry on the phone. Such a wonder-ful feeling. It was very precious. Lisa's home! So proud of her 'too cute' baby. Part of her name will be Olivia … Can't wait to see her.

Things to delight and remember. Read the inscription on Seamus Heaney's latest book.

'In the everything flows and steady go of the world.'

Lovely line. (It's about a perch!) In the everything flows and steady go of the world – I think of you, remember you, love you, adore you so. Another poem refers to Michael Collins – I remembered our visiting his birthplace last year. And it was good and warming.

Your ring close to my heart is such a comfort. I fondle it, kiss it, press it to my lips. Tonight Pat and Phelim Donlon had me in for a meal and a chat, a listen to Phelim's jazz collection, a cigar and a cognac. Pat is a wonderful friend. When I asked Phelim if he would play the piano for me, he played 'Moonlight Sonata' and 'Send in the Clowns'. Were you turning the pages or what? It drew me closer and closer to you.

So, my love, in the everything flows and steady go of the world, I am – like the perch – 'on hold' with you, for you, through you. The dam has burst and my God! – is the seed in my heart blossoming??

And now there's little Olivia. Fruit of the fruit of our love. Hope she looks like you, is you. What a start in life that would be? Your photo rests on my lap. Your ring rests on my lips. Peace. Love. You. You. You. Nothing else matters. Olive. All love. My precious one.

All my love,
John x

17

The End
of the Adventure

At the end of April 2001, Olive and I returned to Otterbrook. It was an emotional homecoming for Olive. Nine months previously, she had left home to go up to Dublin for routine tests which would take no more than a couple of days. On her second day in hospital, she suffered severe haemorrhaging and ended up having a hysterectomy – a more than serious operation in her case, given her respiratory problems. That was only the beginning of the nightmare. Five weeks in hospital and nursing home, and then back to Bray to convalesce. Her sister, Derry, broke her shoulder in a fall, and had to be hospitalised for an operation. Olive and I looked after her. The plan was that we would be home in Galway for Christmas.

Two weeks before Christmas, Olive fell down the stairs in Derry's apartment and broke her neck. She spent Christmas, and the next three months, in hospital, her head encased in that awful 'halo'. To complicate matters, she lost her swallow in the trauma of the fall, and had to be fed by tube directly into her stomach. The medical team were also concerned about her balance when she began to walk again. It was a bleak scenario, but Olive Quinn was always a fighter. Slowly, she edged her way back, recovering her swallow with the aid of a wonderful young speech therapist, and finally shedding the 'halo' in March. Three further weeks in a nursing home and finally back to Bray. Four days later, her beloved sister Derry succumbed quite suddenly to the emphysema. Trauma upon trauma. When Olive was strong enough, I took a month's leave from work, and took her back to Otterbrook.

12.15 a.m.,
Saturday, 25th August, 2001,
Otterbrook,

My darling,
Christ, it's hard coming back here with no you. I bawled for the first thirty minutes. Everything here is you – furniture, new floors, paintings, silver, china. What will I do with all this stuff? More to the point, what will I do without you? Miss you so much – especially here, Couldn't hack it at all at first. Went out and cut the grass and then wrote a poem about your presence here. Calmer now. I suppose it is your presence. I said to you earlier that if I didn't feel you, sense you, hear you, I would just fall apart. I really feel I would …

Played the little snatch of cassette tape from the Navan days when the children were small. It was so lovely to hear your voice – even your little 'Hmmms'– although it made me desperately lonely.

I need you all about me, all the time, always loving me – is that being greedy? Just a measure of how much I love you. Visited your grave on the way down here. I know you're not there – it's just a point of contact – but it only magnified my love and my loss. Rang Lisa tonight. Eva Olivia has settled a bit more and is just 'too cute'. Can't wait to see her, but I know I'll fall to pieces when I do – because I'll be thinking of you and loving you, which I do with all the intensity, tenderness and depth which I can muster. With all my soul, I give myself to you, my beautiful one, my only one.

John x

As I mowed the lawn at sunset
Did I see you
Give a little wave
On returning from your walk?

Did I see you
Move about the kitchen
Making your 'tup of tea'?

Did I watch you
Watch the sun set
From your conservatory chair?

Did I smile
As you gesticulated
To a friend on the phone?

Did I notice you
Glide past the window
With a little glass
Of Muscadet?

And when the dark descended
And I came in
Exhausted
Did I hear you call out
'If you're making
A tup of tea
I wouldn't mind another' …?

Of course I did –
But when I went to make it,
The dark was all around …

May is my favourite month of the year, and it was good to be in Otterbrook for that month. It was a special time for us. We were closer than we had been for a long time, moving at our own pace, enjoying freedom and quiet. Olive built up her strength with daily walks and nightly glasses of Guinness. We lived royally on the wine and champagne I had stocked up for the Christmas we never had. We went out for meals. We were at ease with each other and with life. It was a special time, cherished all the more in retrospect. It was meant to be.

By the time I returned to work in June, Olive had recovered sufficiently to lead an independent life again. She was able to drive the car, do her shopping, enjoy the peace of her beloved Otterbrook. On her birthday, 16th June, I wrote on her card, 'To Molly Bloom, Love and Happiness, Miracle Girl!' Truly, she was a miracle girl. There was no one like her. Mindful of how we had 'postponed' Christmas, I booked us into Kelly's Hotel in Rosslare for a week later in the month. When I told her, she was like a child at Christmas. 'Don't tell anyone where we're going,' she said excitedly.
'Why not?' I asked.
'I just want it to be our secret.'
It was just like old times.

12.50 a.m.,
Sunday, 25th August, 2001,

My darling,
Just back from Henehan's barbecue. Very pleasant – loads of food and drink – but my heart wasn't really in it (guess where it was!) I was anxious to leave when Ann McDonagh arrived and what happened was so wonderful. She is so perceptive …
    'Olive for me was ethereal. She was not for this planet at all, not tuned in to our wavelength. She was just passing through and is now where she needs to be … an angel without wings … my image is of her wearing long flowing clothes … gliding through a crowded room … the hair perfect, the fine chiselled features … she is on a different level now … very content and very close to you …'

It was so wonderful, so real. I told her what I had been through. She understands the 'damburst', what Lois (whom she knows) remembers. So comforting, so reassuring. I am so indebted to her and told her so repeatedly. Her reply?

'There is no such thing as coincidence. Everything is meant to happen at a particular time. I wasn't going to come here tonight, but I changed my mind. When I did come, I didn't know you would be here. It was meant to be.'

O my ethereal one, I am so happy about that. No one but Ann had that perception of you. She is especially gifted. Where does that leave you? This reminds me of meeting your angel in Stephen's Green ... As I said to Ann, wasn't I lucky? Yes — and no! Luck had absolutely nothing to do with it. It was meant to be! I am so uplifted. Thank you, Ann, for such insight.

'And there will be further insights, little ways forward, revealing more and more to you. Hold on to that beautiful love.'

Thank you, my beautiful ethereal one. I was so low going down to Henehan's. Ann transformed me. You organised it. I know that. As Marie Barrett said, nothing will be a problem any more. I love you, my precious one. It was meant to be. Deo Gratias.

All my love — always,
John x

1.45 a.m.,
Thursday, 30th August, 2001,

My darling,
Poetry rules this day. I was given a wonderful poem — 'Watercolour for a Widower' — by Aidan Matthews. I was so deeply touched. It demands several readings but it's a wonderful sea-poem, echoing my own feelings: 'sea of love, sea of loss'.

> This, the last birth and the most bitter,
> Will taste of salt wind and sand dunes forever ...

but it is balanced by the coming of our grand-daughter –

> an olive branch
> Washes in on a warm wave
> From a saltwater uterus …

Exquisite! As Aidan predicted

> My eyes fill up and fulfil
> with something strange and saline …

How often they have filled up, my love, and have burned and stung …

Then I bought Douglas Dunn's 'Elegies' (as recommended by John O'Donohue). In one poem, he 'sieves through' twenty years with his beloved until he reaches,

> 'The truth that waits for me with its loud grief.'

I too sieve – through thirty-five years of presence, to help me cope with absence. Next I came across a little book of Joan Walsh Anglund's poems that I gave you in 1968. I had especially marked for you the lines:

> Just beyond my wisdom are words
> Which would explain everything …

Is that uncanny or … or is it just another one of those little steps that Ann McDonagh mentioned? Probably! Beyond understanding, beyond wisdom – indeed. I must be patient. Wait. Accept the 'not knowing'.

Help me, my darling,
John x

WATERCOLOUR FOR A WIDOWER

for John

Your wife floats out to sea and is lost
In a real swimsuit, in actual surf.
This, the last birth and the most bitter,
Will taste of salt wind and sand dunes forever
With the medical stench of the ocean's ointment.

Shorelines, outlines, waterlines:
The wet mess they once called the margin.
You stand with your two feet on the ground,
Your toes bedded in hard strand
Like a climber's slowly slipping grip …

Even Sherpa Tenzing and Hillary
In their face-masks and oxygen tanks
Traced at the holy pinnacle
The fossils of starfish in the snow clouds
To go with a jetty twenty miles inland.

Now a grand-daughter, an olive branch,
Washes in on a warm wave
From a saltwater uterus
Among girls in white hospital gowns,
Angels with steel oxygen cylinders.

You are the shell of the man you once were.
Put your ear to its aperture.
Listen to the sea that it came from:
Sea of love, sea of loss,
The Aral Sea, the Red Sea, the Sea of Atlantis.
As they lift the child and lower her in,

Her fontanel streaming like Mesopotamia,
Will it be any wonder at all,
Salt-of-the-earth man, gilly of the middle-ground,
That even your eyes fill up and fulfil

With something strange and saline –
Like the tupperware flask of sea-water
I brought home with me from the Mediterranean
And kept on my desk like a skull for a year
Before giving it back to the basin?

(Aidan Matthews)

10.50 p.m.,
Tuesday, 11th September, 2001,
London,

My darling,
*Here I am – and your grand-daughter is gorgeous! Too cute, as Lisa
would say. I think (hope) she has your eyes. Lisa says she definitely can
arch her eyebrows like you did when you were cross.*
*But, just as I walked into Lisa's apartment, an awful atrocity was
unfolding in New York and Washington … Seemed like Armageddon.
I can't really talk about it. All I know is I'm glad you're out of such a
world. It would be too much for you, too distressing. I recall writing
to you when Robert Kennedy was assassinated – we were of one mind,
but couldn't speak. So I'm glad you are safe and removed from all of
this – even if it means you are removed from me. Holding Eva Olivia
was bittersweet – how you would dote over her! Can't get those poor
people in the Twin Towers out of my mind. Can't get you out of my
mind. Would I want to? A black, black day in world history. Hold me.
Together we will triumph. We are one.*
'We two will sit alone like birds i' the cage.'

I love you so very much. That conquers even the blackest day. Thank you, my beautiful one.

John x

2.10 p.m.,
Friday, 14th September, 2001,
Victoria Station,

My darling,
Just back from an amazing trip to Selsey to interview Sir Patrick Moore. What a crazy evening! We had a family of four visitors as 'audience' for most of the interview! The interview was done in bits and pieces but it was wonderful. Patrick is a loveable rogue who lost his loved one to Hitler sixty years ago. It still hurts, so he knows how I feel. Then the neighbours arrived, especially the 'mad Irishwoman' (Patrick's words) Eileen Nolan. And the whiskey flowed – and I had no lunch … Eileen reaffirmed your presence – 'she is here now, glorifying in all of this'. I know you would enjoy the fun … Too much for me! Patrick prepared a lovely dinner and insisted I stay the night. By the time we reached the coffee, I was fading fast, had to excuse myself and retire to bed. Gone in ten seconds! You were probably mortified but – admit it – you would probably have been the same yourself!

Dreamt of you briefly. I threw a book towards you in disgust over something, but apologised later when I took you in my arms and said, 'I love you so very much.' Nice! Patrick had a lovely breakfast ready for me. He is the perfect host. I went for a walk on Selsey Beach where I wrote a poem to you.

Today is a World Day of Mourning for America's lost ones. At 11 a.m. I stood by Patrick's observatory and thought of them – and you – and how infinitesimal this planet is in the scheme of things. And how much hatred and futility there is on it. Like I said, you are well off out of it – only I still miss you like crazy.
John x

On Selsey Beach
I think of you
As I listen to
The symphony of the sea.

On Selsey Beach
I pray for you
And that we two
Will share eternity.

On Selsey Beach
I long for you
To walk with me
Along the pebbled shore.

On Selsey Beach
I call to you
And sing my love
To the ocean's echoing roar.

12.20 p.m.
Tuesday, 18th September, 2001,

My darling, my beautiful bride of 33 years, my love,
This is the day. This is the day you made me so proud and happy. This
is the day I slipped the ring on your finger and promised to love, honour
and obey, in sickness and in health, till death do us part. And now it
has – and that ring nestles close to my heart. Made a bags of that
promise at times, but we stuck at it. All that 'stuff' that got in the way
is gone now. I can see clearly now. You are in perpetual light and wis-
dom. You know now.

I can see clearly that all I ever wanted was your happiness. That's
all. Ever. Ever. Ever. I was so young and innocent then but I know one
thing. You were for me and I was for you. That's why our wedding day

was so wonderful. I never enjoyed a wedding like it. You were so, so beautiful. When I reflect now that you did all the organising yourself – you who had been at death's door two years earlier – you were brilliant. So beautiful, so radiant, so poised, so calm. Thank you for the memories. I was not worthy. Truly I wasn't.

Such wonderful memories. Your late arrival (car wouldn't start!), walking down the aisle, the reception, my singing 'Try to Remember', escaping to Blessington, your missing cosmetics bag (Temper! Temper!), our first gentle night together. Try to remember indeed. I don't have to, my precious one. It's all there. And as the song says, I will follow.

7 p.m., Galileo's Restaurant,
Nice meal. Brandy and soda in our honour. Looking through the album, especially at the wedding photo. To be honest, I can't look at it. You're just – ethereal. Christ, what was I doing there at all? I was so honoured that you chose to commit your life to me. I was as indescribably happy then as I am indescribably lonely now.

I live only for the day when we can be together again – forever, with no 'stuff' in the way. If that's not feasible, there's no point. I might just as well crumble to pieces here in London town. I have never felt the depth of emotion I feel now. It is pure love – absolutely pure – exhilarating and heart-breaking at the same time. Thirty-three years ago this evening I held you in my arms and everything in this world was perfect. Now you are beyond this world and I wait – impatiently – but I wait. How wonderful it will be.

Later still!
Just home from The Phantom of the Opera. *Wonderful production. Of course I cried all the way through 'our song' – 'All I Ask of You' – but it was a good way to celebrate our anniversary. Didn't we have a good time? The seed in my heart continues to blossom – wonderfully, beautifully.*

All my love, always,
John x

Epilogue

Wednesday, 31st July, 2002,

When I go back to Otterbrook now, I make straight for the black leather coat [not the original one, of course!] *that hangs on the hook just inside the door. I caress its soft material, inhale your scent that still clings to its sleeves, and say, 'Here I am, Eddie Duchins.' The tears flow.*

Here I am indeed, and where are you? The great mystery. 'There', I hope, happy, blissfully eternally happy [all I ever wanted for you was to be happy, remember?] *but 'here' too. I believe in your presence – totally. That's why I talk to you all the time.* [Yeh! Yeh! I know – much more than I ever did when you were alive.] *That's why I write con-stantly to you – not that you need my letters now. You know it all now. You are in the light. It's me that needs the letters. I need, desperately, to be in touch with you. I need your presence. That's why I recognised you in St Stephen's Green when the down-and-out whispered in my ear, 'The seed in your heart shall blossom.' You and he were right, of* course. The seed of love has blossomed wonderfully, beautifully, in my heart – and it continues to blossom. Thank you, my darling. It's the strangest mixture of feelings. I am at once heartbroken by your absence and totally consumed by your 'presence' – more in love with you than I ever thought possible.

Is it so with you? Please love me. I know you give me little signs now and then and I know I must be patient. That's the hardest part. A wise man said long ago 'Amor est Passio' *(Love is Suffering)* and he was right!

It's a hard and lonely road without you and while family and friends have been supportive (especially wonderful friends I have made since you died), ultimately it's a road I must walk alone. I miss you – even to argue with! I miss you, terribly, frighteningly. And I need you, now more than ever. So please stay close to me – as close as your wedding ring which I now wear on a chain around my neck – or else I fall apart.

Love you. Miss you. Above all, above all, thank you. Thank you for walking into my life 36 years ago – and staying in it, especially when, occasionally, you must have been tempted to walk out of it! We had our highs and our lows but, in the general mystery of life, we did alright, Eddie Duchins. We did more than alright. Don't know about you, but I'd do it all again!

Of all the throat-swab joints in all the world, you had to walk into mine, swish that black leather coat and flash that smile …

Deo Gratias

John

And it was lovely then
And you were lovely then
And we were young
And so in love
And it was lovely then

– And will be so again
And will be so again …

Permissions

ALL I ASK OF YOU
from THE PHANTOM OF THE OPERA
Music: Andrew Lloyd Webber
Lyrics: Charles Hart
Additional lyrics: Richard Stilgoe
© copyright 1986 The Really Useful Group Ltd.
Reproduced by permission.
All Rights Reserved.
International Copyright Secured.

I HAVE A DREAM used by permission of Bocu Music Ltd.
Composers B. Andersson/B. Ulvaeus.